THE IMPERIAL TREASURY OF THE INDIAN MUGHULS

other recent books from Cosmo Publications . . .

THE HINDUS. *Bestseller*
Encyclopaedia of Hinduism in 5 Volumes
Edited by Subodh Kapoor

ENCYCLOPAEDIA OF INDIAN HERITAGE. in 90 Volumes
A Descriptive Work of Indological Research in Philosophy, Religion, Sacred Literature, Society, Thought, Traditions, and Ancient Sciences.
Edited by Subodh Kapoor

ENCYCLOPAEDIA OF POLITICAL IDEOLOGIES.
in 10 Volumes *Bestseller*
Edited by Gettel, R. G. & Dunning, W. A.

THE INDIAN ENCYCLOPAEDIA
Biographical, Historical, Religious, Administrative, Ethnological, Commercial, and Scientific
in 25 Volumes *Bestseller*
Edited by Subodh Kapoor

ENCYCLOPAEDIA OF INDIAN RULERS.
in 10 Volumes (Ist Series)
Ed. W. W. Hunter

Also Available . . .

INDIAN HISTORICAL RESEARCHES *Bestseller*
By Several Authors of International Repute
in 78 Volumes

LANDMARKS IN INDIAN ANTHROPOLOGY *Bestseller*
By Several Authors of International Repute
in 74 Volumes

REDISCOVERING INDIA *Bestseller*
INIDAN PHILOSOPHY LIBRARY
By Several Authors of International Repute
in 71 Volumes

THE IMPERIAL TREASURY OF THE INDIAN MUGHULS

BY

ABDUL AZIZ

BAR-AT-LAW

SET IN TWO VOLUMES

VOLUME 2

COSMO PUBLICATIONS

2009 New Delhi

THE IMPERIAL TREASURY OF THE INDIAN MUGHULS

First COSMO Print 2009

ISBN 978-81-307-0950-5 (Set)
ISBN 978-81-307-0952-9 (Volume 2)

Published by
MRS. RANI KAPOOR
for COSMO PUBLICATIONS Div. of
GENESIS PUBLISHING PVT. LTD.
24-B, Ansari Road, Darya Ganj,
New Delhi-110 002, INDIA
Ph.: 327 8779, 328 0455
Fax : 324 1200

Printed and bound in India

SECTION III : SAPPHIRES

Linschoten has the following :—

'The Safiers are of two sortes, one of a darke blew, the other of a right [light] blew, the Iacinth, Granades, and Robasses are likewise certaine kinds of Rubies, but little esteemed, the Indians call them the yellow and carnation Rubies, and so foorth, according to their colour.' These 'Iacinthes, Granadoes, and Robasses,' he adds, are common and cheap. 'The Safier is not of so great estimation as the Rubie, and yet is one of the most precious stones that are next the Diamond, and the Rubie'. Of rubies, sapphires and other stones aforesaid, those that come from Pegu, 'are esteemed the finest, whereof there is great store' (II, 140).

Of sapphires, says Fryer, 'there are three sorts, one perfect Blue, and very hard, which if cut of a Diamond-Cut, and without *Calcedone*, is of very good Esteem, and worth a good Price, if it be in perfection.

The second is perfect White, and very hard, which if without blemish, Diamond-Cut, is likewise in Esteem.

TABLE I.—RUBIES WHICH ENTERED

No.	Description	Weight of Cut Stone
		AKBAR'S
1	Standard Ruby.	284 *ratīs*
2	Offered by Rāja Rāmchand of Bhatha to Akbar.	
3	Sent by Prince Dāniyāl to Akbar. ..	104 *ratīs*
		JAHĀÑGĪR'S
1	Presented by Jahāñgīr to Prince Parwīz.	
2	Offered by Āṣaf Khān to Jahāñgīr. ..	
3	Presented to Jahāñgīr by "Mīrza Ḥusain."	
4	Ruby Ring in one piece sent to Jahāñgīr by Murtaẓá Khān from Gujarāt. Of good colour, substance and water.	37 *ratīs*
5	Ruby sent by same.	59 *ratīs*
6	*Quṭbī* Ruby offered by Vazīr Khān. ..	..
7	Offered by Āṣaf Khān to Jahāñgīr. Of beautiful colour and well-shaped.	168 *ratīs*

Price	Authorities
REIGN	
Rs. 100,000	*A'in*, I, 12; Blochmann, 16.
Rs. 50,000	Budāyūnī, II, 335.
	A. N., III, 816; Tr., III, 1224.
REIGN	
Rs. 25,000	*Tūzuk*, 37; R. & B., I, 77.
Rs. 40,000	„ 50.
Rs. 100	„ 56; „ I, 118.
Rs. 25,000*	„ 63; „ I, 132.
„ „	„ „ „ I, 133.
„	„ 70; „ „ I, 147.
Rs. 60,000	Abū'l-Qāsim bought it in Cambay for Rs. 75,000. *Tūzuk*, 70; R. & B., I, 148.

TABLE I—RUBIES WHICH ENTERED

No.	Description	Weight of Cut Stone
8	Bestowed by Jahāñgīr on Prince Parwīz.	
9	Celebrated Ruby offered by Rānā Amar Singh to Prince Khurram, and by the latter to Jahāñgīr. It came originally from Rāja Māldeo.	192 *ratīs*
10	*Quṭbī* Ruby presented by I'timādu'd-Daula to Jahāñgīr.	
11	Ruby of the purest water and brilliance offered by Prince Khurram.	
12	Exceedingly beautiful and clear Ruby offered by Prince Khurram to Jahāñgīr at Ajmir.	
13	Offered to Jahāñgīr by Mahābat Khān.	
14	Sent by Jahāñgīr to Shāh Sulṭān Khurram.	
15	Purchased by Mahābat Khān from a European and offered to Jahāñgīr.	286 or 291½ *ratīs*
16	Fine Ruby offered by Prince Shāh Jahān to Jahāñgīr. Largest in the Treasury.	456 *ratīs*
17	Very fine Ruby of good colour offered by Prince Shāh Jahān to Nūr Jahān.	132 *ratīs*

THE MUGHUL TREASURY—(*Cont.*)

Price	Authorities
,, ,,	*Tūzuk*, 75; R. & B., I, 156.
,, ,,	,, 140; ,, I, 285-86.
Rs. 22,000	,, 156; ,, I, 318.
Rs. 80,000	,, 157; ,, I, 320.
Rs. 60,000	,, 158; ,, I, 32[illegible].
Rs. 65,000	,, 163; ,, I, 333.
Over Rs. 30,000	,, 189; ,, I, 382.
Rs. 100,000	,, 195; ,, I, 394.
Rs. 200,000	Bought at Goa. *Tūzuk*, 198; R. & B., I, 399 40[illegible]
Rs. 50,000	*B. N.*, I, [illegible]i, 189.

TABLE I.— RUBIES WHICH ENTERED

No.	Description.	Weight of Cut Stone
18	Ruby of one colour bestowed by Jahāñgīr on Prince Shāh Jahān. Akbar's mother had presented it to Prince Salīm at the latter's birth.	221 *ratīs*
19	Ruby on Nūr Jahān's necklace. ..	
20	A very fine *qutbī* Ruby offered by Prince Shāh Jahān to Jahāñgīr.	72 *ratīs*
21	Offered by Āṣaf Khān to Jahāñgīr. ..	300 *ratīs*
22	An engraved Ruby of Timurid family sent by Shāh 'Abbās of Persia to Jahāñgīr; then bestowed by the latter on Prince Shāh Jahān. This history engraved on it in three inscriptions. Later set in the middle slab of the rail of the Peacock Throne.	288 or 312 *ratīs*
23	Offered by Lashkar Khān. ..	
24	Offered by Khān Jahān.	
		SHĀH JAHĀN'S
	Central Ruby of Shāh Jahān's *sarpech*. Superior in quality even to the much heavier stone, No. 16 of Jahāñgīr.	288 *rati's*

THE MUGHUL TREASURY (*Contd.*)

Price	Authorities
Rs. 125,000	*Tūzuk*, 202-3; R. & B., I, 409.
Rs. 10,000	,, 263; ,, II, 74.
Rs. 40,000	,, 265; ,, II, 78.
Rs. 125,000	,, 266-67; ,, II, 81.
Rs. 100,000	,, 325; ,, II, 195-96; *B. N.*, I ii, 80.
Rs. 4,000	*Tūzuk*, 326; R. & B., II, 197.
Rs. 100,000	,, 373; ,, II, 281.
REIGN	
Rs. 200,000 or more.	*B. N.*, II, 391

RUBIES WHICH ENTERED THE

No.	Description	Weight of Cut Stone
		AURANGZEB'S
1	Bright coloured Ruby sent by 'Abdu'l-'Azīz Khān of Bukhāra to Aurangzeb.	
2	Sent by 'Ādil Khān of Bījāpur to Aurangzeb.	125 *ratis*
3	Offered by Husain Pāsha, the ruler of Basra.	

Table II.—INDIAN RUBIES WHICH NEVER

No.	Description	Weight of Cut Stone
1	Ruby which belonged to the King of Bījāpur. 'It is hollowed from beneath [i.e. cut *en cabochon*], clean, and of the first quality.'	16 4/5 Engl. car.
2	A Ruby of the second quality. In form an almond *cabochon*, somewhat hollowed beneath, and bored near the point.	58 *ratis*=48½⅝ Engl. car.
3	A Ring with a perfect Ruby which Tavernier presented to Nawāb Ja'far Khān.	

MUGHUL TREASURY—(*Contd.*)

Price	Authorities
REIGN	
Rs. 40,000	'*Ālamgīr Nāma*, 638.
Rs. 20,000	*Ma'āṣir-i-'Ālamgīrī*, 82.
" "	" " 86.

ENTERED THE IMPERIAL TREASURY

Price	Authorities
Rs. 49,700 (1653)	Tavernier, II, 101 and 348 (Pl. IV, Nos. 3 and 4).
Rs. 50,000	A Banian merchant showed it to Tavernier at Benares. Tavernier, II, 102 and 348 (Pl. IV, No. 5).
£ 97 10s.	Tavernier, I, 114.

Some of the world's famous rubies are tabulated

Table III.—FAMOUS RUBIES (*Nos. 1—7 from ruby*

No.	Description	Weight When uncut
1	Ruby, rich in colour; was originally cushion-shaped.	37 carats
2	Ruby, a blunt drop in form. ..	47 carats
3	A colossal stone. Broken into three pieces: Two were cut and the third was sold uncut in Calcutta.	400 carats
4	Another large stone broken into two parts.	
5	A beautiful Ruby, found in Tagoung-nandaing Valley; perfectly clear and of splendid colour.	18½ carats
6	Ruby found in 1899. ..	77 carats
7	Ruby as large as a pigeon's egg. ..	
8	*Shāh's Ruby*. Belongs to the King of Persia. 'It is of the thickness and shape of an egg, is bored through and of very high colour, beautiful and clean, with the exception of a small flaw at the side.'	

here to give a scale of sizes and values.

mines near Magok, near Mandalay, Upper Burma).

Weight When cut	Price	Authorities
32 5/16 carats 38 9/16 carats	£ 10,000 £ 20,000	Brought to Europe in 1875. According to Streeter the finest that ever came to Europe.
The weights of the cut pieces: 70 carats and 45 carats	Price of the third piece, sold uncut: 7 lakhs of rupees =£46,667.	
98 carats 74 carats 11 carats	Sold for £7,000. Now valued at £10,000.	
		Sold in India (1904) for 4 lakhs (£26,667).
		Was presented in 1777 to the Czarina Catherine by Gustav III of Sweden when on a visit to St. Petersburg. Was amongst the Russian regalia.
192 *ratis*= 161 7/25 Engl. car.		Tavernier, II, 100 and 348 (Pl. IV, No. 1).

The third, called Water-*Saphires*, are of small Esteem, being not so hard as the other, and commonly of a dead Waterish Colour; they are of a slender Value' (II, 146).

Jahāṅgīr

In XII R. Y. 'Ādil Khān sent to Jahāṅgīr a sapphire weighing 6 *tānks* and 7 *surkhs*, *i. e.*, 151 jewellers' *rat s*, and valued at Rs. 100,000. The Emperor says he had not seen before such a large and fine sapphire, nor one of such a beautiful and rich colour.[1]

In XIII R. Y., again, on Thursday, the 17th *Sha'bān*, I'timādu'd-Daula presented an offering of a *quṭbī* sapphire exceedingly delicate.[2]

Aurangzeb

Tavernier saw in Aurangzeb's Treasury 'an oriental topaz [yellow sapphire (corundum)] of very high colour cut in eight panels, which weighs 6 melscals [*misqāls*], but on one side it has a small white fog within' (Tavernier, I, 318-19). This, in all probability, was the only jewel which Aurangzeb wore on his cap when he ascended the throne (*Ibid.*, 296).

---

[1]*Tūzuk*, 198.
[2]*Tūzuk*, 237; R. & B., II, 23.

This stone is illustrated as No. 6 of Pl. IV, where the author adds that he did not see the Emperor wear any other jewel during the time he remained at his court on his last visit to India. It weighed 152 4/25 Engl. carats, and was bought at Goa for the Great Mogul for Rs. 181,000 or £20,412 10*s*. (*Ibid.*, II, 102 and 348).

Bernier is probably speaking of the same stone in the following passage : 'The King appeared seated upon his throne, at the end of the great hall, in the most magnificent attire. His vest was of white and delicately flowered satin, with a silk and gold embroidery of the finest texture. The turban, of gold cloth, had an aigrette whose base was composed of diamonds of an extraordinary size and value, besides an Oriental topaz, which may be pronounced unparalleled, exhibiting a lustre like the sun' (Bernier, 268).

Tavernier also saw in Aurangzeb's Treasury an oriental amethyst, *i.e.*, a purple sapphire, strung in the middle of a chain of pearls and emeralds—a long table, weighing some 40 *ratis* (See pp. 307 and 312 below).

TABLE I.—SAPPHIRES IN

No.	Description	Weight of Cut Stone
		JAHAṄGĪR'S
1	Sent by 'Ādil Khān to Jahāṅgīr. Large and fine. Of beautiful and rich colour.	151 *ratis*
2	*Qutbī* sapphire offered by I'timādu'd-Daula to Jahāṅgīr. Exceedingly delicate.	
		AURANGZEB'S
1	The favourite 'Oriental Topaz' of Aurangzeb. Of very high colour. Cut in eight panels. 'Unparalleled.'	152 4/25 Engl. car.
2	The 'Oriental Amethyst' in the middle of Aurangzeb's chain of pearls and emeralds. A long table. 'Perfection of beauty.'	40 *ratis*

Price	Authorities and Remarks
REIGN	
Rs. 100,000	*Tūzuk*, 198; R. & B., I, 400.
	„ 237; „ II, 23.
REIGN	
Rs. 181,000	Bought at Goa for the Emperor. Tavernier, I, 296, 318-19; II, 102 and 348. Bernier, 268.
	Tavernier, I, 318.

TABLE II.—INDIAN SAPPHIRE

No.	Description	Weight of Cut Stone
1	A *Yāqūt-i-kuḥlī* (Budāyūnī) or *Yāqūt-i-arzaq* (Firishta) plundered by Maḥmūd at Muttra in 409 *A.H.*=1018 *A.C.*	450 *misqāls* (!!) or 400 *misqāls*

TABLE III.—FAMOUS

No.	Name or Description	Weight When uncut
1	By far the most gigantic ever reported.	951 carats (cut?)
2	"Rospoli." Quite flawless. ..	132 1/16 carats
3	2 in. long and 1½ in. thick. ..	
4	A fine cut stone, brilliant-cut above, and step-cut below, the girdle.	
5	Image of Budha cut out of a single sapphire, mounted on a gold pin.	

OUTSIDE MUGHUL TREASURY

Price	Authorities and Remarks
	Budāyūnī, *Muntakhab-u't-Tawārīkh* '15; Engl. Transl., I, 25. *Tārīkh-i-Firishta* (Nawalkishor), p. 29. The weight, whether 450 *misqāls* or 400 *misqāls* be taken as the correct tradition, is incredible. It comes to well over 2 seers or 4lb. Nor is such a stone heard of at any later time.

SAPPHIRES

Weight When cut	Price	Remarks
		Seen in 1827 in the treasury of the King of Ava.
		Two splendid rough specimens in the Jardin des Plantes collection (Paris).
100 carats		In possession of Duke of Devonshire.
		In Mineral Gallery of the British Museum (Natural History).

SECTION IV : EMERALDS

Emeralds, says Linschoten, 'there are none throughout al India, yet it is reported yt some have bin found there, but [verie] few & not often : but they are much brought thether from Cairo in Aegypt, and are likewise called Orientall : they are much esteemed in India, because there are but few of them.'[1]

Akbar

Abū'l-Faẓl quotes Rs. 52,000 for an emerald weighing 17¾ *tānks* and 3 *surkhs*, *i.e.*, 429 jewellers' *ratis* (*Ā'īn*, I, 12 ; Blochmann, 16).

Jahāṅgīr

Among the offerings of Ibrāhīm 'Ādil Khān already spoken of was an emerald. 'Although it is from a new mine,' says Jahāṅgīr, 'it is of such a beautiful colour and delicacy as I have never before seen.'[2]

Rāja Bikramājīt, one of Prince Shāh Jahān's favourite officers, on the occasion of being sent

---

[1]Linschoten, II, 140.

[2]*Tūzuk*, 198 ; R. & B., I, 400.

on an expedition to Kangra fort (XIII R. Y.) offered to Jahāṅgīr a string of emeralds worth 10,000 rupees. [1]

From an entry on p. 77 of *Letters Received*, I, we learn that the cost price of two emeralds was £16.

Three emeralds were sold for 3000 rupees (February, 1625).[2]

A Sūrat letter dated 22 December, 1622, records the sale of two emeralds for 2,910 rupees.[3]

From another letter dated 18 June, 1625, we learn that the jewellers valued certain emeralds weighing 40 *ratis* each at four to five rupees the *rati*; but they could not be sold at that price.[4]

Aurangzeb

Tavernier saw in Aurangzeb's Treasury a chain of 'pearls and emeralds, round and bored.

---

[1] *Iqbālnāma-i-Jahāṅgīrī*, 117; *Tūzuk*, 238; R. & B., II, 26.

[2] *E. F. I.* 1622-1623, p. 178.

[3] *E. F. I.* 1622-1623, p. 178.

[4] E. F. I. 1624-1629, p. 89

TABLE I.—EMERALDS IN

No.	Description	Weight of Cut Stone
		AKBAR'S
1	Standard Emerald.	429 *ratīs*
		JAHĀÑGĪR'S
1	Sent by ' Ādil Khān to Jahāñgīr. Fine and of good colour.	
2	String of Emeralds offered by Rāja Bikramājīt to Jahāñgīr.	
		AURANGZEB'S
1	Large Emerald of the 'old rock'. Cut into a rectangle. Of high colour, but with many flaws.	30 *ratīs*

TABLE II.—EMERALDS OUTSIDE

No.	Description	Weight
1	Two Emeralds.	
2	Three Emeralds.	
3	Two Emeralds.	

THE MUGHUL TREASURY

Price	Authorities
REIGN	
Rs. 52,000	*Ā'īn*, I, 12 ; Blochmann, 16.
REIGN	
	Tūzuk, 198 ; R. & B., I, 400.
Rs. 10,000	„ 238 ; „ II, 26 ; *Iqbāl Nāma-i-Jahāngīrī*, 117.
REIGN	
	Tavernier, I, 318.

THE MUGHUL TREASURY

Price	Authorities
£16 for both	*Letters Received*, I, 77.
Rs. 3,000 for three	*E.F.I.* 1622-1623, p. 178.
Rs. 2,910 for both	„ „ „

TABLE III.—FAMOUS

No.	Description	Weight When uncut
1-5	Five choice stones (the so-called Spanish or Peruvian emeralds) presented by Cortez to his bride. These stones had been worked to divers fantastic shapes.	
6	Largest single crystal known to exist at present. Diameter, 2 in.; length, about the same. Of good colour, but badly flawed.	
7	A fine, though much smaller, crystal, but of even better colour. Widest cross-diameter, 1 1/8 in.; length, same.	
8	Finest cut emerald.	
9	Small but perfect and flawless, faceted emerald. Set in a gold hoop.	

EMERALDS

Weight When cut	Price	Remarks
		Lost in 1529, when Cortez was shipwrecked.
1347 carats		In possession of the Duke of Devonshire. Exhibited at the Great Exhibition of 1851.
156½ carats		In Mineral Gallery of the British Museum (Natural History).
30 carats		Belonged to the Czar of Russia.
		In British Museum (Natural History). See illustration in Smith, *Gem-stones*, Pl. I, fig. 5.

All the pearls are round', he says, 'and of diverse waters, and from 10 to 12 ratis each in weight.' In the middle of this chain there was 'an oriental amethyst [*i.e.*, a purple sapphire], a long table, weighing about 40 ratis, and the perfection of beauty' (Tavernier, I, 318).

In the middle of the chain of rubies already spoken of (under Rubies) there was a large emerald of the "old rock", cut into a rectangle, and of high colour, but with many flaws. It weighed about 30 *ratis* (*Ibid.*).

A journalistic item may close our account of the emeralds: The theft of an emerald valued at 5 lakhs of rupees from the Bahawalpur State treasury was reported in the *Civil and Military Gazette* of Lahore, dated 23 February, 1938. The editor's current comment, which appeared in the next day's issue, runs as follows:—'The loss of an emerald worth Rs. 5 lakhs (or nearly £37,000) from the collection of His Highness the Nawab of Bahawalpur will remind many of the fact that His Highness possesses some of the finest emeralds in the world. In India, the emerald has always occupied a very high place among precious stones, even higher than the diamond, and connoisseurs have always been willing to pay a very high price for emeralds of the best quality, higher than even the price of diamonds weight for weight. It is the colour that decides the quality of the emerald. Stones of the velvety green colour are rare.'

SECTION V: TOPAZ

'The Topaz,' says Fryer, 'is a Stone very hard, full as hard as the *Saphire*; some are very yellow, and like the Colour of Muskadine, pleasant to look on, which bears a good Price if good and without fault. The Stones may be burnt white in the Fire, and look very well. Another sort are said to be white naturally, which would bear a good Price if perfect, and cut of the Diamond-Cut. There's another sort of them soft, yet shew very well, but have not the quickness of the other, and therefore of low esteem; trial of their hardness may be made by a *Saphire* or such a Stone' (II, 147).

FAMOUS

No.	Name or description	Weight When uncut
1	"Braganza."	1680 carats
2	Large rough crystal of opaque Topaz. ..	137 lb.

TOPAZ

Weight. When cut	Price	Remarks
		In the Portuguese regalia. Supposed to be a diamond but probably a white topaz, says Mr. Smith (p. 170). The *New Standard Dictionary* treats it as a diamond; and the *Encyclopaedia Britannica* article apparently counts it as a topaz (VI, 764).
		From a felspar quarry in Norway. In mineral collection of British Museum (Natural History) (*Encyclopaedia Britannica*, XXII, 297).

SECTION VI : *YĀQŪTS* (?HYACINTH)

Yāqūts present some difficulty. The definitions in the dictionaries are vague and not helpful. Etymologically, *yāqūt* is the same word as jacinth or hyacinth (Gr. *hyakinthos*).[1] According to Steingass it means 'a hyacinth, a ruby, a cornelian; any precious stone;' and the equivalents given in Salmone's *Arabic-English Dictionary* are 'jacinth; ruby; sapphire; chrysolite'. This information is not definite; and does not carry us far. But what is a hyacinth (or jacinth)? It means '(1) Formerly, a bluish-violet gem, probably the sapphire. (2) Now, in jewelry, usually brownish, reddish, or orange zircon, but sometimes cinnamon-coloured garnet; essonite; also, occasionally applied to honey-yellow pyrope garnets' (*New Standard Dictionary*). Again a hyacinth or jacinth is 'a variety of zircon of yellowish red colour, used as a gem-stone. The *hyacinthus* of ancient writers must have been our sapphire, or blue corundum, while the hyacinth of modern mineralogists

---

[1] See Ovington (pp. 260-61 above), who is supported by Steingass.

may have been the stone known as *lyncurium.* The Hebrew word *leshem,* translated ligure in the A. V. (Exod. xxviii. 19),..........appears in the R. V. as jacinth, but with a marginal alternative of amber ; both may be reddish yellow, but their identification is doubtful. Most of the gems known in trade as hyacinth are only garnets, generally the deep orange-brown hessonite or cinnamon stone ; and the stones known as Compostella hyacinths are simply ferruginous quartz from Santiago de Compostella, Spain. Hyacinth is not a common mineral' (*Encyclopaedia Britannica,* XI, 954).

When no definite meaning can be assigned to 'hyacinth', what purpose can be served by explaining *yāqūt* as a hyacinth?

R. & B. translate *yāqūt,* as jacinth in some places,[1] and as ruby in another.[2] Again they render red *yāqūt* as a ruby,[3] blue *yāqūt* as a sapphire,[3] and yellow *yāqūt* as a topaz.[4] Here

---

[1] R. & B., I, 132 and 396.

[2] R. & B., II, 78.

[3] R. & B., II, 200.

[4] R. & B., I, 318 and f. n. 2.

apparently they follow the lead of Linschoten,[1] Ovington[2] and the rest. The *Makhzanu'l-Adwia* has an article on *yāqūt*, written apparently under western influence, where a similar classification is countenanced.

Blochmann & Phillott are more cautious, and, without committing themselves by adopting an equivalent, let *yāqūt* stand as it is.[3]

In the *Jawāhirnāmas*, we find that a *yāqūt* is not a kind of ruby, or sapphire or topaz, but is recognized as a distinct mineral, and has a place among the major precious stones. *Yāqūts*, we are told, are of four kinds; red, blue, yellow and white. The blue *yāqūts*, again, are divided into five varieties, the yellow ones into four, and the white ones into seven. And all these varieties are named.[4] *Ghyāsu'l-Lughāt*, drawing apparently upon some other *Jawāhirnāma*, gives seven varieties of the red *yāqūt*, whereas

---

[1] P. 289 above.

[2] P. 260 above.

[3] *Ā'īn*, I, tr., p. 16.

[4] *Jawāhirnāma* printed in *Oriental College Magazine* for August, 1928, Part I, pp. 112-32.

our *Jawāhirnāma* gives none. But these coincide with those of the white *yāqūt* in our *Jawāhirnāma*.

Again, we are told that crystals of hyacinth (*i.e.*, zircon) are rare, and not large enough for cutting.[1] But the reader has seen that Shāh Jahān had two rosaries which had altogether 125 pearls strung alternately with coloured *yāqūts*—total value, 20 lakhs of rupees. These *yāqūts* must have been of respectable size and high value. Further, the reader will find several important single *yāqūts* mentioned below. It is difficult to identify these valuable *yāqūts* with hyacinth, which is an insignificant stone.

Fryer has the following: 'The Hyacinth is a Stone Yellow and Transparent; it's of the hardness of the *Emerald*; these Stones are naturally foul, and full of little Sands like Gold; if they be in Perfection, and of a very good Colour, they bear a reasonable Price' (II, 147).

---

[1] *Encyclopaedia Britannica* article cited above.

I suspect the classification of the Persian writers differs radically from that of the modern mineralogists in many respects. Occasional remarks made by Linschoten,[1] Ovington,[2] Tavernier and others point to the same conclusion. This will account for much of the uncertainty and confusion that envelop this subject.

In consideration of all these facts I have thought it safe to adopt *yāqūts* as a heading and have collected under it all mentions of that stone, the Persian name being preserved throughout.

Akbar

The *Ā'in's* quotation for a *yāqūt* of 4 *tānks* and 7¾ *surkhs, viz.,* 103¾ jewellers' *ratis* is Rs. 50,000 (*Āīn'*, I, 12; Blochmann, 16).

Jahāngir

Some *yāqūts* figure among presentations of Āṣaf Khān on one occasion.[3]

---

[1] See p. 289 above.

[2] See pp. 260-61 above.

[3] *Tūzuk*, 63; R. & B., I, 132.

Among the presents offered by Mīr Jamālu'd-Dīn Husain early in XI R. Y. was a jewelled dagger which he himself had got prepared. On its hilt was set a yellow *yāqūt* very clear and fine, the size of half a hen's egg, along with other *yiqūts* of pleasing colours and old emeralds of remarkable shape and cut. The emperor adds that such a fine and big yellow *yāqūt* has never been seen. The appraisers fixed the price of the dagger at Rs. 50,000.[1]

By yellow *yāqūt* in this passage R. & B.[2] understand a topaz, and by *yāqūt* a ruby. For this and other reasons I have chosen to give my own translation.

In XII R. Y. Jahāṅgīr bestowed on Rāja Bharjīv of Bāglāna three rings of *yāqūt*, diamond and ruby.[3]

A *yāqūt* of good colour, water and shape, weighing 22 *ratīs*, was offered by Prince Shāh Jahān to Jahāṅgīr (XIV New Year's Day). It was valued at Rs. 40,000.[4]

---

[1] *Tūzuk*, 155-56.

[2] R. & B., I, 317-18.

[3] *Tūzuk*, 196; R. & B., I, 396.

[4] *Tūzuk*, 265; R. & B., II, 78

Jahāngīr says that he sent to Shāh Parwīz by the hands of Rāja Sārang Deo a *khāṣṣa* dress of honour, with a jewelled belt, which bore one blue and a few red *yāqūts*. R. & B. have translated the former as sapphire, and the latter as ruby.[1]

Shāh Jahān

It is recorded in the annals of IX R. Y. of Shāh Jahān's reign that the Emperor sent 'Abdu'l-Laṭīf of Gujarāt to Quṭbu'l-Mulk at Golconda demanding the payment of a heavy tribute in gems and jewelled things and elephants; and Nihāl Chand, jeweller, was sent along with 'Abdu'l-Laṭīf to help in selecting and appraising the precious stones. The day when Quṭbu'l-Mulk came out to receive Shāh Jahān's *farmān*, the jeweller noticed on Quṭbu'l-Mulk's finger a *yāqūt* ring of rare beauty. And when the treasure sent by Quṭbu'l-Mulk was displayed before the Emperor, the ring was mentioned by the two officers. Afzal Khān was at once ordered to

[1] *Tūzuk*, 327; R. & B., II, 200.

write to Qutbu'l-Mulk asking for the ring. Qutbu'l-Mulk sent it without delay. The *yāqūt* was found to weigh 12 *ratīs*, had a beautiful colour, and was pure. It was consequently approved, and the price of it, which was fixed at Rs. 50,000, was credited to Qutbu'l-Mulk in his *Peshkash* account (*B. N.*, I, ii, 209).

SECTION VII: PEARLS

'The Pearles,' says Linschoten, 'are sold by sives which are made of [mettell driven into thin plate][1] for that purpose, whereof the holes are round. There are many sorts of sives, the first hath small holes, and the Pearles that passe through them are at one price: the next sive hath greater holes, and the Pearles that fall through it are at higher price, and so foorth [at the least] seaven or eight sives. The small stuffe that serve for no Pearles, they call Alioffar, and are sold by the ounce, and used by Potticaries and Physitions, and to that end many of them are caried into Portingall, & Venice, and are very good cheape. To give the Pearles a faire colour, in India they use rice beaten a little with salt, wherewith they rub

[1]Orig. Dutch: 'blik' (white iron)

YĀQŪTS IN THE

No.	Description	Weight
		AKBAR'S
1	Standard *Yāqūt*.	.. 103¾ *ratis*
		JAHĀÑGĪR'S
1	*Yāqūt* of good colour, water and shape, offered by Prince Shāh Jahān to Jahāñgīr.	22 *ratis*
		SHAH JAHĀN'S
1	*Yāqūt* in Quṭbu'l-Mulk's ring, pure and of beautiful colour.	12 *ratis*

IMPERIAL TREASURY

Price	Authorities
REIGN	
Rs. 50,000	*Ā'īn*, I, 12 ; Blochmann, 16.
REIGN	
Rs. 40,000	*Tūzuk*, 265 ; R. & B., II, 78.
REIGN	
Rs. 50,000	*B. N.*, I, ii, 209.

them, and then they become as faire and cleare as christall, and so continue' (Linschoten, II, 135).

We learn from Manucci that Arabian and Persian vessels brought to India seed-pearls, pearls, and Jew's stones[1] (*Storia*, I, 59).

Manucci thus describes the seed-pearl fisheries of Tuticorin, and the way they were worked :

'Since I am speaking of that coast, I will state how they obtain seed-pearls on the shores of Tutochorim (Tuticorin) and in Manār. The inhabitants know the time of year for removing the pearls. It is in the months of March and April. The Dutch, as lords of the sea-shore on the coast of Tuticorin, and of the coast of Manār in the island of Ceylon, give licenses to fish for twenty-one different days. In this way they begin at the end of March, and spread the fishing out to May 20 or thereabouts. In this fishery participate six hundred *toni* (Tamil, *tōni*), which are vessels sufficient

[1] '*Lapis judaicus* (considered a diuretic and dissolvent of calculus).'-Steingass.

for the purpose. Every vessel has a crew of thirty men, who pay the Dutch six *patacas* [=12 rupees] a head if they are Christians, nine if Hindû, twelve if Mahomedans. The Christian boats are three hundred, those of the Hindûs one hundred, and of the Mahomedans two hundred. Added together, these come to eighteen thousand men. These are the divers. Many more people collect as traders, carriers, including women and children. Ordinarily, during the fishing season there are forty thousand people. Each vessel pays one *pataca* for a *cartajo* (a license or permit). All this money together amounts to one hundred and forty-four thousand three hundred *patacas*.[1] Besides this, the Dutch provide supplies of rice, pulses, salted fish, and flour, *et cetera*, for sale to all this crowd. From this they derive great profit, for they sell at whatever prices they like.

The way of obtaining the seed-pearls is as follows: These vessels anchor in ten, twelve, or even sixteen fathoms. The divers

---

[1] *I* make the total come to 143.600 *patacas*.'—Editor's footnote.

are naked and oiled all over. In entering the water they lay hold of a rope, at the end of which a stone is attached, and this helps them to get nearer the bottom.[1] Another separate rope is tied round the man's waist. He has a basket hung across his shoulder, and holds in his hand a *coita* [bill-hook] which he uses to detach any shells which may be stuck to stones. Thus he rapidly fills the basket, and this done, he shakes the rope round his waist. His companions in the vessel, on getting this signal, haul him up as fast as they can to the surface, and take the shells. The diver who went down first takes a rest, and another man takes his place. Thus they continue the whole day, taking it in turns, and in the evening they withdraw, and from every boat they collect the shells and put them in a place set apart for them.

Some merchants take the chance of buying unopened oysters, the highest price given being one *pataca* per thousand. If the oysters turn out not to be rich in pearls, they do not

---

[1] 'The Venice Codex XLIV. adds that a weight is fastened to the diver's feet.'—Editor's footnote.

lose their money; while some have such good fortune as to enrich themselves at the cost of one *patara*. The fishing being over, they leave the oysters to rot, and the smell makes anyone ill who is present. They leave the oysters to decay, because in this way the pearls turn out of a better colour, and the Dutch as over-lords of the site purchase the best, and at the cheapest rates. Every year at this fishery there die without fail a considerable number of the divers while diving.'[1]

There is a similar account in Linschoten (II, 133-35).

Akbar

The standard price given in *Ā'īn* is Rs. 50,000 for a pearl weighing 5 *tānks*, which means 120 jewellers' *ratis* (*Ā'īn*, I, 12; Blochmann, 16).

Jahāñgīr

We have already seen (pp. 265-66 above) that Jahāñgīr presented a necklace consisting of four rubies and one hundred pearls to Prince Parwīz (I R. Y.).

---

[1] *Storia*, III, 106-8.

Again, a ruby and two single pearls valued at about Rs. 40,000 were bestowed on Prince Khurram in IV R. Y. (p. 268 above).

Some five months later, Khān Khānān sent to Jahāṅgīr a ruby and two pearls of the value of about Rs. 20,000 (*Ibid.*).

On the New Year's Day of V R. Y. Khān-i-A'ẕam offered a pearl worth Rs. 4,000.[1]

Here is a good example of a gift of low-priced pearls on a large scale : ' As I had made a rule', says Jahāṅgīr, 'that they should bring before me after two watches of the night had passed the dervishes and necessitous people who had collected in the illustrious palace, this year also after the same manner I bestowed on the dervishes with my own hand and in my own presence 55,000 rupees and 190,000 bighas of land, with fourteen entire villages, and twenty-six ploughs, and 11,000 *kharwār*[2] (ass-loads) of rice ; I presented as well 732 pearls, of the value of 36,000 rupees, to the

---

[1] *Tūzuk*. 79 ; R.& B., I, 165.

[2] A *kharwār*, lit., an ass-load, was a weight equal to 100 Tabrīzī maunds or nearly 700 lb. English.

servants who by way of loyalty had bored their ears.'[1]

In X R. Y. Rāi Sūraj Singh received a pair of pearls for his ears (pendants apparently); and another pair of pearls was sent to Khān Jahān.[2]

We have also already learnt (pp. 269-70 above) that among Dayānat Khān's offerings (XI R. Y.) there were two pearl rosaries and six large pearls, though their price is not separately marked.

The next day I'timādu'd-Daula offered, among other things, two pearls worth Rs. 30,000 (*Ibid.*).

Salāmulla, the Arab, received a *ḥalqa* of pearls.[3] What is meant is not clear. R. & B. construe a *ḥalqa* as a necklace; but an ear-ring would suit the context better.

The story has already been narrated of a grand pearl worth Rs. 20,000 which Muqarrab

---

[1] *Tūzuk*, 136-37; R. & B., I, 279.

[2] *Tūzuk*. 144; R. & B., I, 293.

[3] *Tūzuk*, 157; R. & B., I, 320.

Khān had procured for Jahāñgīr, and for which Prince Khurram found a match in an old *sar-pech* of Akbar's time. We need only refer here to pp. 270-72 above.

Among 'Ādil Khān's offerings came (XII R. Y.) two pearls, one weighing 64 or 65 *surkhs* and valued at Rs. 25,000, and another weighing 16 *surkhs*, very round and fine, valued at Rs. 12,000.[1]

Muqarrab Khān came from Ahmadābād and offered a pearl which he had bought for 30,000 rupees.[2]

We have already noticed (p. 276 above) how on a hunting expedition to Amānābād Nūr Jahān broke her necklace and lost a ruby worth Rs. 10,000 and a pearl worth Rs. 1,000.

Among the offerings brought forth by Prince Shāh Jahān on the XIV New Year's Feast were six pearls: one of these, which Shāh Jahān's agents had bought in Gujarāt for Rs. 25,000,

[1] *Tūzuk*, 198; R. & B., I, 400.

[2] *Tūzuk*, 206; R. & B., I, 415.

weighed I *tānk* and 8 *surkhs*, or 32 *ratis* ; while the other five were altogether worth Rs. 33,000.[1]

On Sunday, the 4th *Farwardin*, XIV R. Y., Khān Jahān invited Jahāngīr to an entertainment. He offered valuable presents, out of which the worth of 1,30,000 rupees including a pearl, which he had bought for 20,000 rupees, was accepted.[2]

The following story of how a pearl was lost and found is not only relevant here but is interesting as a curiosity of occult knowledge : 'It is a strange thing that when a pearl of the value of Rs. 14,000 or 15,000 was lost in the harem, Jotik Rāy, the astrologer, represented that it would be found in two or three days. Ṣādiq K. Rammāl (soothsayer) represented that in the same two or three days it would come from a place which was perfectly clean and pure, such as the place of worship or oratory. A female soothsayer represented that it would soon be found, and that a woman

[1] *Tūzuk*, 265 ; R. & B., II, 78.
[2] *Tūzuk*, 266 ; R. & B., II, 80.

with white skin would bring it in a state of ecstasy, and give it into the hand of the Ḥaẓrat (the king). It happened that on the third day one of the Turkish girls found it in the oratory, and all in smiles and in a happy frame of mind gave it to me. As the words of all three came true each one was favoured with an acceptable reward. This is written because it is not devoid of strangeness.'[1]

A merchant sold to Nūr Jahān two large pearls, which he had brought from Turkey, for 60,000 rupees. One weighed 1¼ *misqāls* or 33 *ratīs* and the other one *ratī* less, *i.e.*, 32 *ratīs*. The empress offered the pair to Jahāṅgīr.[2]

A pearl was sometimes used as a button (*tukma*). A dress with a *nādiri* having *tukmas* of pearl was bestowed on Prince Shahryār,[3] Prince Parwīz,[4] and Khān Jahān.[5]

---

[1] *Tūzuk*, 346 ; R. & B., II, 235.
[2] *Tūzuk*, 347 ; R. & B., II, 237.
[3] *Tūzuk*, 347 ; R. & B., II, 237.
[4] *Tūzuk*, 377 ; R. & B., II, 288.
[5] *Tūzuk*, 380 ; R. & B., II, 295.

A simple string of pearls frequently passed as a present in this reign: A rosary worth 10,000 rupees was bestowed on prince Parwīz (*Rajab*, 1018);[1] one on Bakhtar Khān *kalāvant* (*Dai*, IX R. Y.);[2] another one of valuable pearls was conferred on Khurram (*Isfandārmuz*, IX R. Y.);[3] another worth 50,000 rupees on Rāna Karan;[4] and yet another on Jagat Singh, son of Rāna Karan (29 *Tir*, XVIII R. Y.).[5]

The following two items are of more than usual interest, and deserve individual attention:

Jahāṅgīr tells us that *'iṭr* of roses (otto of roses) was invented in his reign by the mother of Nūr Jahān. After describing the method of its preparation, and its superior qualities, the emperor adds that in recognition of this achievement he bestowed on the inventress a

---

1 *Tūzuk*, 75; R. & B., I, 157.
2 *Tūzuk*, 133; R. & B., I, 271.
3 *Tūzuk*, 136; R. & B., I, 278.
4 *Tūzuk*, 144; R. & B., I, 293.
5 *Tūzuk*, 367; R. & B., II, 270.

string of pearls. The *'iṭr* was given the name *'iṭr-i-Jahāñgīrī*.[1]

On the occasion of the anniversary of Ḥaẓrat Khwāja Mu'īnu'd-Dīn Chishtī, which fell on Sunday, 13 *Amurdād*, X R.Y., Jahāñgīr visited the Khwāja's tomb (at Ajmir). 'On the night of Sunday, as it was the anniversary of the great Khwāja,' says the emperor, 'I went to his revered mausoleum, and remained there till midnight. The attendants and Sufis exhibited ecstatic states, and I gave the fakirs and attendants money with my own hand; altogether there were expended 6,000 rupees in cash, 100 *saub-kurta* (a robe down to the ankles), 70 rosaries of pearls, coral and amber, etc.'[2]

Among offerings: Rustam Khān offered a rosary of pearls (17 *Farwardīn*, X R. Y.),[3] and Mukarram Khān came from the province of Orissa with a similar present.[4]

---

1 *Tūzuk*, 132-33.
2 *Tūzuk*, 146; R. & B., I, 297.
3 *Tūzuk*, 139; R. & B., I: 283.
4 *Tūzuk*, 332; R. & B., II. 208-9.

Sir Thomas Roe, writing from Aḥmadābād in December, 1617, says that he has sold the great pearl for 12,000 [*khazāna*] rupees, which was equivalent in value to 10,000 *Jahāṅgīrīs*. He adds that the pearl was worth a little more, but he could not find a purchaser, and so indulged Āṣaf Khān for reasons of policy.[1]

John Company's servants once bought some pearls at a total cost of £1521 17s. On being brought to Jahāṅgīr's court, they were rejected by Āṣaf Khān. They were then offered to Muqarrab Khān, but were 'disgraced in the Kings presence by Assuff Can, as being his refuzalls' (*E. F. I.* 1618-1621, p. 9). After having been unsuccessfully offered to many people, they were finally sold in June, 1618, to Āṣaf Khān for Rs. 8,092—at considerable loss (Roe, 450, f. n. 1). Sir Thomas Roe takes them to task for such ruinous dealings. He exhorts them either to buy cheaper or to invoice their goods right. The ambassador assures them that at the prices scheduled by him, a yearly sale to the value of £50,000

[1] *Letters Received*, VI, 230 ; Roe, 424.

ready money is possible, if pearls of good weight and beauty were chosen; and, further, that a trade of similar volume could be driven in precious stones, if bought according to his specifications (Roe, 450).

Sūrat factors, writing on 18 February, 1620, speak of a great pearl which has been received and sent up to the court, and add that pearls are esteemed rather by their greatness than their beauty.[1]

A Sūrat letter dated 7 November, 1621, informs us that the great pearl, which cost £340, was sold for Rs. 5000.[2] Perhaps this is the pearl referred to in the previous paragraph.

A pair of pendant pearls was sold for 2,300 rupees (February, 1625).[3]

Shāh Jahān

At the time of the treaty between Shāh Jahān and Qutbu'l-Mulk, the latter asked for

---

[1] *E. F. I.* 1618-1621, p. 185.
[2] *E. F. I.* 1618-1621, p. 328.
[3] *E. F. I.* 1622-1623, p. 178.

the Emperor's portrait. The Emperor had one sumptuously framed in pearls, and furnished with a string of precious pearls to hang it by. He sent it to him with other things including a tablet of gold on which the terms of the treaty were inscribed.[1]

In the passage quoted at length from 'Abdu'l-Ḥamīd's *Bādshāhnāma* (p. 283 above) we have already seen that S͟hāh Jahān's celebrated *sar-pech* (turban ornament) comprised besides five rubies twenty-four large pearls. The best and the largest of these, we were told, was of the shape of a guava, weighed 47 *ratis*, and was valued at Rs. 50,000.

Next to this *sar-pech* came the *tasbiḥ* on which there were thirty pearls and five rubies—total value, 8 lakhs of rupees (*Ibid.*).

The two other *tasbiḥs* already referred to comprised 125 pearls. These rosaries, which contained pearls and coloured *yāqūts*, were priced at 20 lakhs; and the central pearl of each was valued at Rs. 40,000, and weighed 32 *ratis* (*Ibid.*).

---

[1] *B.N.*, I, ii, 210.

Shāh Jahān sent one lakh of rupees through Mīr Ibrāhīm Ṣafdarkhānī to Ma'dīna, to be paid to Imām Qulī Khān, who had been shamefully ill-treated by his younger brother, Nazr Muḥammad Khān of Tūrān, and who was now visiting the Holy places. Imām Qulī Khān, it so happened, died at Madīna before Mīr Ibrāhīm reached there. The latter thought it best under the circumstances to invest the money in purchases; so he bought from 'Alī Pāshā, governor of Laḥsā, a guava-shaped pearl weighing 43 *surkhs* for Rs. 30,000, besides some Arab horses.

On 21 *Ramazān*, 1054 *A.H.*, Ibrāhīm Ṣafdarkhānī came back to Court and waited on the Emperor. The pearl was approved and placed on the famous *sar-pech*, the price being fixed at 40,000 rupees (*B. N.*, II, 390-91).

We have it in the *Bādshāhnāma* that on the occasion of Jahān Ārā's recovery from a long illness lasting 8 months and 8 days, a feast of rejoicing was held from the 5th to the 12th of *Shawwāl*, 1054 *A. H.*, the bath of recovery taking place on the last day of *Ramaẓān*. On the opening day of the feast the Emperor bestowed on her 130 unbored pearls for a *dast-band* (bracelet), the value totalling 5 lakhs of rupees (*B. N.*, II, 396-97).

On Solar Weighment (10 *Rabi'* I, 1065) Jahān Ārā Begum's presents to the Emperor included a pearl weighing 31 *ratīs*, which the princess had bought for 40,000 rupees.[1]

On the same occasion Shā'ista Khān offered presents worth two lakhs of rupees, including a large pearl which weighed nearly 46 *ratis* and was valued at 40,000 rupees.[1]

In a letter of April 13, 1630 we read: ' You shall doe well to continew your resolves for sending noe more jewells, except rare and ritch pearles, wherein the King taketh most delight. Other sortes hee doth nott esteeme, nor indeed of any thing, if not very curious, substantiall, and ritch.'[2]

Aurangzeb

On 7 *Shawwāl*, 1071, Būdāq Beg, the Persian ambassador, offered to Aurangzeb his master's

---

[1] *B.N.*, III, f. 96*b*; *A.S.*, III, 199.
[2] *E.F.I.* 1630-1633, p. 22.

presents—total value, 4,22,000 rupees. These included a bright, round pearl weighing 37 carats, such as is rarely met with (as the historian assures us). The royal connoisseurs appraised it at 60,000 rupees.[1]

On 24 *Sha'bān*, 1082, Muḥammad Amīn Khān offered 280 pearls valued at 1,05,000 rupees.[2]

Tavernier has a long note on pearls he found in Aurangzeb's Jewel Treasury: When inspecting it he saw 'two grand pear-shaped pearls, one weighing about 70 ratis, a little flattened on both sides, and of beautiful water and good form. Also a pearl button, which might weigh from 55 to 60 ratis, of good form and good water. Also a round pearl of great perfection, a little flat on one side, which weighs 56 ratis. I ascertained this to be the precise weight,' he continues, 'and that Shāh Abbās II, King of Persia, sent it as a present to the Great Mogul. Also three other round pearls, each of 25 to 28 ratis, or thereabouts, but their

[1] *'Alamgīr Nāma*, 622; *Ma'āsir-i-'Alamgīrī*, 36.

[2] *Ma'āsir-i-'Alamgīrī*, 113.

water tends to yellow. Also a perfectly round pearl of 36½ ratis, of a lively white, and perfect in every respect. It is the only jewel which Aurangzeb, who reigns at present, has himself purchased on account of its beauty, for the rest either came to him from Dārā Shikoh, his eldest brother, he having appropriated them after he had caused his head to be cut off, or they were presents made to him after he ascended the throne. I have elsewhere remarked that the Emperor has no great regard for jewels, priding himself only on being a great zealot of the law of Muhammad.

'Ākil Khān also placed in my hands, for he allowed me to examine all at my ease, two other pearls, perfectly round and equal, each of which weighed 25¼ ratis. One is slightly yellow, but the other is of a very lively water, and the most beautiful that can be seen. It is true, as I have elsewhere said, that the Prince of Arabia, who has taken Maskat from the Portuguese, possesses a pearl which surpasses in beauty all others in the world; for it is perfectly round, and so white and lively that it looks as though it was transparent, but it only weighs 14 carats. There is not a single monarch in Asia who has not asked the Prince of Arabia to sell him this pearl. Also two chains, one of pearls and rubies of different shapes pierced like the pearls; the other of pearls and emeralds, round and bored. All the pearls are round and of diverse waters, and from 10 to 12 ratis each in weight. In the middle of the chain of rubies there is a large emerald of the "old-rock", cut into a rectangle, and of high colour, but with many flaws. It weighs about 30 ratis. In the middle of the chain of emeralds there is an oriental amethyst [purple sapphire], a long table, weighing about 40 ratis, and the perfection of beauty' (Tavernier, I, 317-18).

Corresponding to the Illustration No. 4, Pl. V, we have the following letterpress:

'No. 4 is the figure of a large pearl perfect both as regards its water and its form which is like that of an olive. It is in the middle of a chain of emeralds and rubies that the Great Mogul sometimes wears round his neck, and it hangs down to his waist' (Tavernier, II, 103).

Now Tavernier, in the long passage quoted above, speaks no doubt of a chain of pearls and rubies, and of another chain of pearls and emeralds, but he has spoken nowhere of one of emeralds and rubies. Nor is it likely that here he is speaking of a third chain ; for he himself tells us in letterpress to No. 5 just below[1] that it is customary to place a pearl between two rubies or between two emeralds—which is corroborated by the arrangement of the two chains already spoken of. The truth of the matter is that Tavernier is pleasant easy-chair reading, but once you prick the bubble everything goes to pieces. It appears it wasn't Tavernier's practice to turn back to what he had once written, to compare or to verify. Consistency, we have noticed again and again, is a minor virtue with him.

The following letterpress corresponds to Illustration No. 5 on Plate V :

'As a round pearl of perfect form, this is the largest I know of, and it belongs to the Great Mogul. Its equal has never been found,

[1] See next quotation.

for which reason the Great Mogul has not worn it, but has left it with other jewels which are unmounted. For if a match for it had been found, the pair might have been used as ear pendants, and each of the two pearls would have been placed between two rubies or two emeralds, in conformity with the custom of the country, everyone, rich or poor, in proportion to his means, wearing in each ear a pearl set between two coloured stones' (Tavernier, II, 103-4).

Is this one of the single pearls mentioned by Tavernier in his inspection note, or had he forgotten all about this important pearl ? In any case no cross reference is given to facilitate identification ; and we can only make guesses.

The largest pearl Tavernier saw at the Mughul court was the one which , he says, ' is suspended from the neck of a peacock made of precious stones, and rests on the breast, and this peacock surmounts the throne '. This pearl is illustrated in Tavernier, Pl. V, No. 2 (Tavernier, II, 103).

In the following passage Tavernier speaks of a grand bouquet of nine large pear-shaped pearls, which he presented to Aurangzeb, and goes on to narrate at length the story of the sale of a pear-shaped pearl of 55 Florentine (or $52\frac{4}{5}$ English) carats, which Ja'far Khān tried in vain to buy, and which was finally sold to Shā'ista Khān at a considerable rebate:

'When I arrived at Jahānābād, one of them [*i.e.*, the two Persians, *viz.*, Nawāb 'Āqil Khān "Mīr 'Askarī" and Mīrzā Mu'azzam, and the Banian, Nihāl Chand] came and told me that he had the Emperor's order to see what I brought, before I would be permitted to exhibit it in his presence. They sincerely wished that the Emperor was not at Jahānābād, because they would have tried to buy all that I had for themselves, in order to profit by reselling it to the Emperor, and to the Princes when the opportunity should occur—this, nevertheless, they had never been able to induce me to do.

On the following day all three came to see me, one after the other, and they wished to get from me amongst other things a grand bouquet of nine large pear-shaped pearls, the largest of which weighed thirty carats and the least sixteen with another single pear-shaped pearl of fifty-five carats. As for the bouquet, the Emperor took it; but with regard to the pearl, seeing that, notwithstanding all that they could say, I was, unwilling to sell them anything, they so managed that before I had shown my jewels to the Emperor Ja‘far Khān, his uncle saw it, after which he did not wish to return it, saying that he would pay me as high a price for it as the Emperor, asking me not to mention it; for in fact he desired to present it to the Emperor.

After the Emperor had selected from among my jewels those which he desired, Ja‘far Khān bought several pieces from me, and at the same time purchased the great pearl. Some days afterwards he caused me to be paid the amount agreed upon, with the exception of the pearl, upon which he desired me to rebate 10,000 rupees. The two Persians and the Banian had maliciously informed him that on my arrival they might, if they had wished, have had the pearl for 8,000 or 10,000 less than I had sold it to him for; this was wholly untrue, and Ja'far Khān having told me that if I would not accept the money which he offered me I might take it back, I took him at his word, assuring him that he would never see it again during his life. I kept to my word, and remained firm in my resolve.........

Having then started for Bengal [*i.e.*, Tavernier having then started for Bengal], these three inspectors of jewels, incensed with spite, and urged on, no doubt, by Ja'far Khān, who was anxious to take his revenge for my refusal, wrote to Shāista Khān that I was taking some jewels to show to him, and among others a very beautiful pearl which I had sold to Ja'far Khān; but that he had returned it to me when he ascertained that I was trying to make him pay 10,000 rupees more than it was worth. They wrote similarly regarding the other jewels which I carried, and it was upon these false and malicious advices, which Shāista Khān did not receive till after he had delivered to me my bill of exchange, that the Prince wished to deduct 20,000 rupees from the total sum; this was reduced finally to a rebate of 10,000 rupees, with which I was obliged to content myself' (Tavernier, I, 112-13).

The author informs us in another place (II, 89) that this pearl 'of well-formed pear shape, and of fine water' came from the pearl fishery of the Margarita island. The pearls found there, he says, surpass the others in perfection, both as regards water and size.

This pearl is illustrated as No. 3, Pl. V, where, however, the water is described as 'somewhat dead'—by no means a solitary example of the author's short memory and slipshod manner. It is the largest pearl, he adds, which has ever been taken from Europe to Asia (II, 103).

A few more stories of pearls which never entered the Mughul Treasury to our knowledge are nevertheless interesting. Some or all of these may have found their way eventually into the Imperial Treasury.

Tavernier went to meet Mīr Jumla at Gandikota, and paid a preliminary visit to him on September 3, 1652.

'On the 4th,' he says, 'we again visited the Nawāb, and showed him the jewels which we hoped to sell to the King. They consisted of some pear-shaped pearls of a weight, beauty, and size which were unusual—the least exceeding 24 carats. After having examined them well, and shown them to a number of nobles who were present with him, he asked us the price; which having heard, he returned them to us, and at the same time said he would consider it' (Tavernier, I, 229).

Elsewhere Tavernier narrates the story of a 'large pearl of good water, but badly shaped', which Sh̲ā'ista Kh̲ān had once refused to buy from him. The nobleman asked for it again. Tavernier's report of the transaction is as follows:

'After I had handed it to him, "Say no more about it", said he. "In a word, how much do you want for this pearl?" I asked him 7,000 rupees for it, and it is true that rather than carry it back to France I would have taken 3,000. "If I give you", he replied, "5,000 rupees for this pearl, you will be well repaid for the loss which you say you have sustained on the golden rupees. Come to-morrow and I shall pay you 5,000 rupees. I wish you to leave contented, and you shall have in addition a khil'at and a horse." I then made him a bow, and besought him to give me a young horse, fit for work, as I had a long journey to make. Accordingly, on the following day, I received as he had promised, the robe, mantle, two waistbands, and the turban, which constitute, as I have elsewhere described, the complete suit which these princes are accustomed to bestow upon those whom they desire to honour' (Tavernier, I, 17-18).

The Editor guesses that this pearl was the chief of the pearls Tavernier showed to Mīr Jumla at Gandikota.

Once in the hands of Shā'ista Khān, it may subsequently have found its way into the Imperial collection.

Tavernier has the following story of a pearl belonging to the 'Prince of Muscat': 'This Prince,' he says, 'possesses the most beautiful pearl in the world, not by reason of its size, for it only weighs 12 1/16 carats, nor on account of its perfect roundness; but because it is so clear and so transparent that you can almost see the light through it. As the Gulf opposite Hormuz is scarcely 12 leagues wide from Arabia Felix to the coast of Persia, and the Arabs were at peace with the Persians, the Prince of Muscat came to visit the Khān of Hormuz, who entertained him with magnificence, and invited the English, Dutch, and some other Franks, in which number I was included, to the festival. At the close of the feast the Prince took this pearl out of a small purse which he carried suspended from his neck and showed it to the Khān and the rest of the company. The Khān wished to buy it, to present to the King of Persia, and offered up to 2,000 tomāns [about £6,900], but the Prince was unwilling to part with it. Since then I crossed the sea with a Banian merchant whom the Great Mogul was sending to this Prince to offer him 40,000 écus [£9,000] for this pearl; but he refused to accept that sum' (Tavernier, II, 87).

TABLE I.—PEARLS IN THE

No.	Description	Weight
		AKBAR'S
1	Model Pearl in Akbar's Treasury. ..	120 *ratīs*
		JAHĀṄGĪR'S
1	Offered by " Khān-i-A'ẓam " to Jahāṅgīr.	
2	732 pearls distributed by Jahāṅgīr among his loyal servants.	
3	Two pearls offered by I'timādu'd-Daula.	
4	Grand Pearl procured by Muqarrab Khān for Jahāṅgīr.	
5	"Ādil Khān's offerings : One Pearl. ..	64 *ratīs*
6	Another Pearl. Very round and fine. ..	16 *ratīs*
7	Pearl offered by Muqarrab Khān. ..	
8	Pearl on Nūr Jahān's necklace. ..	
9	Prince Shāh Jahān's offerings : One Pearl.	32 *ratīs*
10	Five other Pearls.	
11	Pearl offered by Khān Jahān. ..	

IMPERIAL TREASURY

Price	Authorities and Remarks
REIGN	
Rs. 50,000	A'īn, I, 12; Blochmann, 16.
REIGN	
Rs. 4,000	*Tūzuk*, 79 ; R. & B., I, 165.
Rs. 36,000 for 732 pearls	,, 136-37 ; R. & B., I, 279.
Rs. 30,000 for both	,, 156 ; ,, I, 318-19.
Rs. 20,000	Another to match it fourd in Akbar's *sar-pech*. *Tūzuk*, 158 ; R. & B., I, 322.
Rs. 25,000	*Tūzuk*, 198 ; R. & B., I, 400.
Rs. 12,000	,, ,, ,, ,, ,,
Rs. 30,000	*Tūzuk*, 206 ; R. & B., I, 415.
Rs. 1,000	,, 263 ; ,, II, 74.
Rs. 25,000	Bought in Gujarāt. *Tūzuk*, 265 ; R.& B., II, 78.
Rs. 33,000 for all the five pearls	
Rs. 20,000	*Tūzuk*, 266 ; R. & B., II, 80.

TABLE I.—PEARLS IN THE

No.	Description	Weight
12	Pearl lost and found in the Haram.	
13	Pair of large pearls bought by Nūr Jahān and presented to Jahāṅgīr.	33 and 32 *ratīs*
14	Rosary of pearls bestowed by Jahāṅgīr on Prince Parwīz.	
15	Rosary of pearls bestowed by Jahāṅgīr on Rānā Karan.	
	SHĀH JAHĀN'S	
1	The best and the largest Pearl on Shāh Jahān's famous *sar-pech*. Of the shape of a guava.	47 *ratīs*
2	The central Pearl of each of the two *tasbīḥs*.	32 *ratīs*
3	Guava-shaped Pearl bought by Mīr Ibrāhīm Ṣafdarkhānī at Madīna.	43 *ratīs*
4	130 unbored Pearls presented by Shāh Jahān for Jahān Ārā's bracelet.	
5	Pearl offered by Jahān Ārā Begum to Shāh Jahān.	31 *ratīs*

IMPERIAL TREASURY (*Cont.*)

Price	Authorities and Remarks
Rs. 14,000 or 15,000	*Tūzuk*, 346 ; R. & B., II, 235.
Rs. 60,000 for the pair	„ 347 ; „ „ 237.
Rs. 10,000	„ 75 ; „ I, 157.
Rs. 50,000	„ 144 ; „ „ 293.
REIGN	
Rs. 50,000	*B. N.*, II, 392.
Rs. 40,000	„ „ „
Bought for Rs 30,000. Official price : Rs. 40,000	„ „ 390-91.
Rs. 500,000 for all the pearls	„ „ 396-97.
Rs. 40,000	*B. N.*, III, f. 96*b* ; *A.S.*, III, 199.

TABLE I.—PEARLS IN THE

No.	Description	Weight
6	Large Pearl offered by Shā'ista Khān to Shāh Jahān.	Nearly 46 *ratīs*
		AURANGZEB'S
1	Bright round Pearl sent by the Shāh of Persia to Aurangzeb.	37 carats
2	280 Pearls offered by Muḥammad Amīn Khān.	
	Seen by Tavernier in Aurangzeb's Treasury:	
3	(a) Pear-shaped Pearl. A little flattened on both sides. Of beautiful water and good form.	70 *ratīs*
4	(b) A Pearl-button. Of good form and good water.	55 to 60 *ratīs*
5	(c) A round Pearl of great perfection. A little flat on one side. Sent by Shāh 'Abbās II to the Great Mogul.	56 *ratīs*
	(d) Three round Pearls. Their water tends to yellow.	25 to 28 *ratīs* each
7	(e) A perfectly round Pearl. Of a lively white. Perfect in every respect. The only jewel purchased by Aurangzeb on account of its beauty.	36½ *ratīs*

IMPERIAL TREASURY (*Cont.*)

Price	Authorities and Remarks
Rs. 40,000	*B. N.*, III, f. 96*b* ; *A. S.*, III, 199.
REIGN	
Rs. 60,000	*'Ālamgīr Nāma*, 622 ; *Ma'āsir-i-'Ālamgīrī*, 36.
Rs. 1,05,000 for 280 Pearls	*Ma'āsir-i-'Ālamgīrī*, 113.
	Tavernier, I, 317-18.

TABLE I.—PEARLS IN THE

No.	Description	Weight
8	(f) Two other Pearls. Perfectly round. One slightly yellow. The other of very lively water, and most beautiful.	25¼ *ratis* each
9	(g) The Pearls on the chain of pearls and rubies, and on that of pearls and emeralds. All the pearls round and of diverse waters.	10 to 12 *ratis* each
10	Large Pearl 'in the middle of a chain of emeralds and rubies'. Perfect as regards water and form. Of the shape of an olive.	
11	Round Pearl of perfect form.	
12	Pearl suspended from the neck of the peacock on the Peacock Throne. The largest pearl Tavernier saw at the Mughul Court.	
13-14	A grand bouquet of nine large pear-shaped Pearls offered by Tavernier to Aurangzeb. The largest of these weighed 30 Flor. carats, and the smallest 16 Flor. carats.	

IMPERIAL TREASURY (*Cont.*)

Price	Authorities and Remarks
	Tavernier, II, 103 (Illustr. No. 4, Pl. V). ,, II, 103-104 (Illustr. No. 5 Pl. V). It may or may not be the same as No. 3 (c) or No. 5 (e) above.
	Tavernier, II, 103 (Illustr. No. 2, Pl. V).
	Tavernier, I. 112.

TABLE II.—INDIAN PEARLS

No.	Description	Weight
1	Pearl sold by Roe to Āṣaf Khān. ..	
2	Great Pearl sold by the E. I. Company factors.	
3	Pair of Pendant Pearls.	
4	Pear-shaped Pearl of fine water which Ja'far Khān tried to buy, and Shā'ista Khān finally purchased from Tavernier.	55 Flor. car. = 52 4/5 Engl. car.
5	Some pear-shaped Pearls of unusual weight, beauty, and size shown by Tavernier to Mīr Jumla.	From 24 Flor. carats upwards
6	Large Pearl of good water but badly shaped, sold by Tavernier to Shā'ista Khān.	

OUTSIDE THE MUG̱HUL TREASURY

Price	Authorities and Remarks
Rs. 12,000 *khazāna* =Rs. 10,000 *Jahāṅgīrī*	*Letters Received*, VI, 230 ; Roe, 424.
Rs. 5,000	*E.F.I.* 1618-1621, p. 328.
Rs. 2,300	,, 1622-1623, p. 178.
Probably a costly article, since a rebate of Rs. 10,000 was asked on it.	Tavernier, I, 112-113, and II, 103 (Illustr. No. 3, Pl. V) and 348.
	Tavernier, I, 229.
Rs. 5,000	,, ,, 17-18. Possibly the chief of the pearls shown by Tavernier to Mīr Jumla(No. 5 above).

TABLE III.—

No.	Description	Weight
1	Largest known pearl. Cylindrical in form, with a slight swelling at one end. Measures 2 in. in length, 4½ in. in circumference about the thicker, and 3¼ in. about the thinner end. About three-quarters of it is white in colour with a fine 'orient,' the remainder bronze in tint (Smith, 294).	454 carats
2	Large pearl.	300 carats
3	Pear-shaped.	
4	"La Pellegrina." Beautiful white Indian pearl. Perfect sphere in shape.	28 carats
5	"Great Southern Cross." 'Consists of nine large pearls naturally joined together in the shape of a cross, was discovered in an oyster fished up in 1886 off the beds of Western Australia' (Smith, 294).	
6	Some pearls of curious shapes.	

FAMOUS PEARLS

Price	Remarks
Over £12,000	Was at one time in Henry Philip Hope's famous collection.
	Was in Imperial crown of Emperor of Austria.
	In possession of the Shāh of Persia.
	In Museum of Zosima in Moscow.
	In Green Vaults at Dresden.

TABLE III.—

No.	Description	Weight
7	The Pearl of the Prince of Muscat. The most beautiful in the world. Round, perfectly clear, and transparent.	12 1/16 or $14\frac{7}{8}$ Flor. carats
8	The largest pearl of which Tavernier had knowledge. The King of Persia bought this in 1633 from an Arab who had just received it from the fisheries at Al-katif. 'It is the largest and most perfect pearl ever discovered, and it has not the least defect.'	
9	The biggest absolutely perfect pearl. The most superb specimen in the world. 'Although its diameter is that of a dime, the pearl is flawless, with a clear, lustrous beauty which excites wonder in all who see it' (Newspaper report, April, 1930).	

FAMOUS PEARLS (*Cont.*)

Price	Authorities and Remarks
More than £9,000	Tavernier, II, 87; and p. 86, f.n. 1.
£110,400	,, ,, 103 (Illustr. No. 1, Pl. V).
$750,000	'Experts with the greatest knowledge of pearls say it is the biggest absolutely perfect pearl they have ever seen. It is certain there is not another like it in the whole world. It is one of nature's miracles. There are pearls in England that are bigger, but in quality cannot equal this one'.—Speech of Captain W. Llewellyn Amos, Secretary, National Jewellers' Association. It was fished by divers in the Persian Gulf, and came by way of India. Now in possession of a London firm. If all this is not mere journalistic sensationalism, this pearl ought to be among pearls what Cullinan (when whole) was among diamonds.

A footnote by the Editor supplements this information as follows: 'The account in the *Persian Travels* is that the pearl belonged to the Amīr of Vodana, who showed it to M. Constant and our author at Hormuz; it was perfectly round and transparent, and weighed 17 'abbās, or 14 7/8 carats, the 'abbās being equal to 7/8 of a carat. On behalf of the Governor of Surat, the latter, on a subsequent occasion, offered 60,000 rupees, say £6,750, to the owner for it, but he refused to sell it (*Persian Travels*, bk. ii, ch. ix)' (P. 86, f.n. 1). We can only add that the discrepancies are irreconcilable and thoroughly characteristic of the author.

CASKETS OF JEWELS

Occasionally we hear of caskets containing jewels being given away as an integral present.

When the imperialists defeated the rebellious Khusrau in I R. Y., his box of jewels and precious things fell into their hands.[1]

---

[1] *Tūzuk*, 30; R. & B., I, 65.

The following presentations are recorded under *Shawwāl*, 1026:[1] 'Ādil Khān sent to Jahāñgīr, through Prince Khurram, a casket of precious stones. Khān Jahān offered a casket full of gems and jewelled things. A parcel of gems and jewelled articles was offered by Mahābat Khān, the value of which was placed at 1,24,000 rupees.

On 21 *Shawwāl*, 1117, Aurangzeb bestowed on Sāhū Jī, son of Sambhājī, a special robe of honour and two valuable caskets. Presumably these caskets contained jewels.[2]

On the occasion of the death of their parents, princes Dādār Bakhsh and Dāwar Bakhsh received a sealed casket containing jewels and a bundle containing *khāṣṣa* dress (17 *Rabīʿ* I, 1118).[3]

SECTION VIII: ROCK-CRYSTAL

'Rock Crystal,' says Mr. Goodchild, 'is the ordinary colourless variety ; it is always crys-

---

[1] *Tūzuk*, 195 ; R. & B., I, 394.

[2] *Ma'āsir-i-'Ālamgīrī*, 511.

[3] *Ibid.*, 515.

talline and often crystallised. The crystals are usually elongated, and of sizes varying from a small pin to several feet in length. Fresange records a crystal from Madagascar measuring 20 feet in circumference. Dauphiné (Bourg d'Oisans) is famous for its groups of Rock Crystal (Fig. 12). The Alps generally have afforded fine specimens, and a notable group in the museum at Naples may be mentioned. In 1719 a cavity was found at Zinken, in the Bernese Oberland, from which crystals weighing altogether 50 tons were taken, and sold for some £60,000, some of the crystals weighing up to 8 hundredweight. In Upper Valais, crystals were found in a cavity which were of extraordinary size, up to over half a ton in weight. The Carrara marble quarries have also afforded good specimens. A specimen in Paris, taken by the French in Italy in 1797, weighs 8 hundredweight and is 3 feet in diameter. The Caucasus, Siberia, Brazil, and particularly Japan, have produced fine specimens. In North America, Moose Mountain, in New Hampshire, may be cited as a locality' (Goodchild, 149-50).

'The fashionable ladies of ancient Rome', continues the same writer, 'used it to cool their delicate hands with, for this purpose carrying small spheres of Rock Crystal in hot weather............

In ancient times it was highly valued, especially perhaps by the Romans, for the production of vases and cups, some of which were of remarkable size, for it is recorded by Ben Mansur that at the capture of Ghasna in 1159 four vases made of Rock Crystal were found, each of which would hold two skinfuls of water. Pliny records that the material then used came from the Alps, and at that time it was believed to be water frozen so hard that it could not be thawed at ordinary temperature; this is said to have led the Romans to only use it for cold liquids. One of the most beautiful pieces of work in this material was a vase belonging to the French Kings; it was 9 inches high and 9½ inches in diameter, and was carved with figures illustrating the intoxication of Noah. It cost some £4,000..................

The Indians seem to have had some secret method of *uniformly* staining Quartz' (Goodchild, 150-52).

Articles made of rock-crystal, both for use and decoration, were in great favour at the Mughul court. In Persian histories we are often coming up against mentions of pure, stainless crystals and articles of all kinds made of them. Cups and other things are of common occurrence. Occasionally we hear of 'looking-glasses' of Aleppo in gold and jewelled cases, and of Venetian crystal boxes and cups.

In his account of Cambaia (*i.e.*, Kambhāyat), Linschoten says: 'They have likewise a kind of mountain Christall, wherof they make many signets, buttons, beades, and divers other devises.'[1]

Yet from a remark by the same writer (II, 138) it appears that rock-crystal was not found in India nor in any other Oriental country. But we are told in Watt, *Dictionary of the Economi Products of India* (II, 170) that rock-crystals are abundant in South India, and are found in the Bombay Presidency and all over the country.

---

[1] Linschoten, I, 61.

On the Fifth New Year's Day, Mahābat Khān offered ' two European boxes, the sides of which were made with slabs of glass, so that whatever was placed inside could be seen from outside in a way that you might say there was nothing between them ' (*Tūzuk*, 79 ; R. & B., I, 165).

Among the articles offered by Prince Khurram to his royal father on one occasion (early in X R. Y.) was, ' a little crystal box of Frank work, made with great taste ' (*Tūzuk*, 140 ; R. & B., I, 286).

' When the merchant ' Abdu-l-Karīm left Iran for Hindustan, my exalted brother Shāh 'Abbās sent me by his hand a rosary of cornelian from Yemen and a cup of Venetian workmanship, which was very fine and rare ' (*Tūzuk*, 152 ; R. & B., I, 310). They were placed before the Emperor on the 9th *Bahman*, X R. Y.

' On the 21st [*Farwardin*, XII R. Y. =1026 *A. H.*],' says Jahāngīr, ' I gave leave to Muhammad Riza, ambassador of the ruler of

Irān, and bestowed on him 60,000 darbs, equal to 30,000 rupees, with a dress of honour. As an equivalent to the souvenir (*yādbūdi*) that my brother Shāh 'Abbās had sent to me, I forwarded with the aforesaid ambassador certain presents of jewelled things which the ruler of the Deccan had sent, with cloths and rare things of every kind fit for presentation, of the value of 100,000 rupees. Among these was a crystal cup that Chelebī had sent from 'Irāq. The Shāh had seen this cup and said to the ambassador that if his brother (Jahāngīr) would drink wine out of it and send it to him it would be a great mark of affection. When the ambassador represented this, having drunk wine several times out of the cup in his presence, I ordered them to make a lid and a saucer for it and sent it along with the presents. The lid was of enamel (*minā-kārī*). I ordered the Munshis of mercurial writing (*'Utārid-raqm*) to write in due form an answer to the letter he had brought' (*Tūzuk*, 185 ; R. & B., I, 374).

'Lately,' writes Roe in a letter to the East India Company dated Ajmīr, 25 January, 1615 [-16], 'the King of Bisampore sent his ambassador with 36 elephants, two with all their chaines of wrought beaten gould, two of silver, the rest brasse, and 40 rich furnished horses, with jewells to the valew of 10 *lecks* of *rupias*; yet withall he sent China wares and one figure of christall, which the King accepted more then that masse of wealth ' (Roe, 99).

On March 12, 1616, Roe was brought before Jahāñgīr, to whom he delivered as a most welcome present 'a purse which cost in England 24*s*., containing "a little boxe of cristall, made by arte like a rubie, and cutt into the stone in curious workes, which was all inameld and inlayde with fine gould. Soe rare a peece was never seene in India, as can wittnes all your servants resident at Adsmere. I can sett noe price, because it was geven me; but I could have sould it for a thousand rupees, and was enformed that had it beene knowne how highlye the King esteemed it, I mought have had 5,000 rupees. The King the same night sent for all the Christians, and others his owne subjects, artificers in gould and stone, to demand if ever they sawe such woorke or howe it could be wrought: who generallie confessed they never sawe such arte, nor could tell how to goe about it, whereat the King sent me woord he esteemed it above a diamonde geven him that day of 6,000 *li*. price.[1]......................Within the boxe (which I presented to keepe the jewells in which others gave him) I putt a chain of gould of double lincks veary small, wheratt was hanged a whyte emrald cutt in the forme of a seale, and therein engraved, no bigger then a penny, a Cupid drawing his bowe, with this motto *Guardes*: being a curiositie not easilie matched, and esteemed by the King for exellent woorke. The stone was unsett, pendent and veary lardge, above halfe an inch in length. The gould wayed 46*s*....... There being noe man in London, much lesse here, that can enamell upon stone, and therfore I knowe not what it [the box] coste ; and the seale stone uncutt, I bought in the West Indies, and had it pollished and carved in London ; it cost noe great matter rough" ' (Roe, p. 127, f.n. I). This seems to be rather an overdrawn picture of an article of considerable beauty and workmanship. There is no mention of it in the *Tūzuk*, however.

[1]There is, however, no mention of this stone in *Tūzuk*.

Among the articles required by the John Company factors for presents, we have 'two or three Venice crystal boxes' (*Letters*, III, 88).

On Thursday, the 13th *Tīr*, XIV R. Y., Sayyid Hasan, the ambassador of Shāh 'Abbās of Persia, placed before Jahāngīr, with a letter from his master 'a crystal drinking-cup, on the cover of which was [set] a ruby' (*Tūzuk*, 273; R. & B., II, 93-94).

Aurangzeb

Tavernier once presented to Aurangzeb 'a battle mace [*gurz* or *shash-par*] of rock-crystal, all the sides of which were covered with rubies and emeralds inlaid in gold in the crystal. This piece cost 3,119 livres [£233 18*s*. 6*d*.] (Tavernier, I, 114).

'I remember seeing the Emperor drink upon three different occasions while seated on his throne,' says the same writer in another place. 'He had brought to him on a golden saucer, enriched with diamonds, rubies and emeralds, a large cup of rock-crystal, all round and smooth, the cover of which was of gold, with the same decoration as the saucer. As a rule no one sees the Emperor eat except his womenkind and eunuchs, and it is very rarely that he goes to dine at the house of any of his subjects, whether it belongs to a Prince or to one of his own relatives' (I, 309-10).

'Vessels made of rock-crystal,' adds the editor, 'were much esteemed by the Emperors. Ball saw some very fine examples of large size which were found in the palace at the capture of Delhi after the Mutiny. Possibly some of the fine specimens preserved in the Green Vaults at Dresden came from India. See Watt, *Commercial Products*, 561 : *Enc. Brit.*, xxiii. 433. Some splendid examples of modern work in rock-crystal are illustrated in *Country Life*, 16th April 1921, p. lxxii' (Tavernier, I, 309, f.n. 3).

The following story from the *Storia* is just worth quoting :

Prince Shāh 'Ālam once ordered Manucci 'to send at once to procure him some crystal vessels for drinking water from. I sent off a man to Bombay to bring some. This order he executed —nay, those he brought were very handsome. These I presented to the prince.

He seemed to be astonished to see so many crystals at once—more than he had ever seen in all his life—for he imagined them to be of rock-crystal, which is extremely costly in the Mogul country. This is the reason of his asking me what the whole might be worth. Quite happy, I answered him that it was a present from me, and that Doctor Nicolas stated no prices to kings' (*Storia*, II, 401). Nor, apparently, did Doctor Nicolas scruple to play tricks on kings when opportunity served. Shah 'Ālam then gave Manucci a valuable set of robes and a very nice horse.

Here is a report from the same source of a rather large crystal found in the Ganges near Patna: 'When Dā'ūd Khān was in charge of Paṭnah, as I have already said (II. 61), there was found one morning in the Ganges river, near the English Factory adjoining the city gate, a rock crystal eight palms in length and thirty palms in circumference. As it was a rarity, it was sent to the king in a boat. I saw it myself, and measured it in the year one thousand six hundred and sixty-three (1663)' (*Storia*, III, 133).

CHAPTER IV

NOTICES OF SEMI-PRECIOUS STONES AND OTHER SUBSTANCES

CHAPTER IV

NOTICES OF SEMI-PRECIOUS STONES AND OTHER SUBSTANCES

We have been able to deal specifically only with the so-called precious stones. It is not to be inferred by any means that the treasury contained no other stones. Probably semi-precious stones went to make up a much larger quantity in the treasury.

One would think that exceptionally good and large specimens of these were assiduously collected and jealously guarded. We have no doubt the treasury contained specimens remarkable for beauty and colour, purity and size, of amethysts, garnets, chrysolites, turquoises, agates, moss-agates, sphenes, jaspers, opals, cornelians, onyxes, sardonyxes, cat's-eyes, corals, chalcedony, lapis lazuli, and vermilion.[1] And presumably there was

1. These names are not chosen at random. I have taken most of them from Fryer's list of 'Precious Stones of the East' (II, 142) and Linschoten's accounts of stones found in various places in India. These I have supplemented with such others as have been actually mentioned by Persian and English historians and other European travellers.

no dearth of such curiosities as the bezoar-stones, the so-called snake-stones, the porcupine stones, and the *yadatāsh* or rain-stones. Nor is this cursory catalogue by any means exhaustive.

We may now take up some of these and string together a few interesting remarks about each made either by scientists who have specialized in the subject or by European travellers like Linschoten, Tavernier and Fryer, who comment on them with special regard to Indian conditions.

AMETHYST

It is a species of quartz, and has beautiful violet, purple or blue shades.

The word is derived from the Greek and means non-intoxicant, testifying to the old belief that the wine drunk out of a cup of amethyst would not intoxicate.

On exposure to heat amethyst generally turns yellow.

'The amethyst was used as a gem-stone by the ancient Egyptians, and was largely employed in antiquity for intaglios it is now used for episcopal rings' (*Enc. Brit.*, I, 807).

This mineral is widely distributed, but good specimens of pure amethyst fit for ornamental purposes are comparatively rare.

'The Amethist,' says Fryer, 'is a Stone of three several Colours, some of them are of a Violet Colour, some are of a more Oriental Colour, therefore called (*Amethist* Oriental) which bears a very good Price, few of these being to be found, but are the pleasantest Colour of all Stones. Another sort being Pale is called the White *Amethist*, or *Amethist* of *Carthagenā*: This naturally is of a quick or sparkling Water, and very good Colour, having for the most part a Blush of Red, which Stones in Perfection bear a tolerable Price' (II, 148).

In *Tārīkh-i-Yamīn* (E. & D., II, 45) we have mention of a stone, which is identified by Mr. Hodivāla[1] as a very fine specimen of amethyst.

[1] *Studies in Indo-Muslim History*, 148.

It weighed 450 *misqāls* or about 4⅔ lb. av. or 5⅝ lb. troy.

AGATE

'In India, Agate is abundantly found in the Deccan rocks in the Kathiawar Peninsula to the West of the Gulf of Cambay, and is largely cut at Cambay (Kanbayat). Also in Rajpipla, and in the Rajmahal Hills' (Goodchild, *Precious Stones*, 170).

The Royal Scottish Museum contains a fine collection of Agates from various places in Scotland.

'There are many purposes besides those of ornament to which this material is put; such are, its use for the knife-edges of chemical balances, for the pivots for marine compasses, in the manufacture of pestles and mortars for grinding hard substances, for burnishing metals, rollers for use in textile industries, dies for moulding plumbago for lead pencils, etc. But by far the greater part produced is wrought into vases, bowls, paper-knives, trays, signet rings, seals, brooches, beads, sleeve links, and other such articles' (*Ibid.*, 170-71).

'Many very beautiful works of art have been produced in this material. France possesses a complete service in Agate, valued at one time at £ 20,000; and many fine examples of this work are to be seen in most of our larger museums' (P. 171).

The price of rough agate runs from £ 5 to £250 per hundredweight according to quality.

The Surat factors say that they can supply Agate or *bābāghorī*[1] beads, and also speak of agate cups which the Ahmadābād factors have sent them (*E.F.I.* 1618-1621, p. 52).

Fryer says (II, 148) that agate is used for handles of knives, which is corroborated by a statement on p. 231 of *E.F.I.* 1637-1641, where we read of a case of knives with agate handles being presented to the king of Bījāpur.

It appears that agate pictures were imported into India and offered for sale both by the East India Company and by the Venetians, for we are told on p. 327 of *E.F.I.* 1618-1621,

---

1 'The white agate of Cambay, so called from the patron saint of the district in which the mines are situated' (*Ibid.*, f.n. 1).

that 'the aggatt pictures come farr shorte of your esteeme of them, by reason of quantities brought in by the Venetians; those that are allready sould of the said aggatt pictures doe produce but fifty per cent. proffitt, whereas in tymes past such yeilded three for one.'

On p. 99 of *E.F.I.* 1668-1669 we read of 'a small agate box containing three cornelian rings' being presented to Lord Arlington.

Moss-agates, which Fryer calls 'Tree-stones,' have, he says, a lively representation or form of a tree on them, and are esteemed (II, 147).

CAT'S-EYE

Cat's-eyes 'come out of Cambaia, but the best out of Seylon and Pegu: they are little brought into Portingal, for there they are not esteemed, and likewise because they are worth more in India then in Portingall, for the Indians esteeme much of them, specially the Chinos, and thether they are caryed, better esteemed, and sold there then any other stones: the Indians say that this stone hath a certaine propertie and vertue to preserve and keepe a man in the riches which he hath, and that they shall not lessen, but stil increase' (Linschoten, II, 141-42).

TURQUOISE

Turquoise 'occurs in various shades of green and blue, sometimes rather grey or white.' The most valued colours among Western races are the rich sky blue, but among many of the Eastern people the more abundant green shades are preferred' (Goodchild, 284). 'The best specimens are known as Oriental Turquois or "stones of the old rock"' (*Ibid.*, 286).

The turquoïses, says Linschoten, 'in India are little esteemed, for that the Indians and Portingals do not weare many of them, and make small account of them.'[1]

'Turquoise occurs only in Persia, and it is obtained in two mines. One of them which is called "the old rock" is three days' journey from Meshed towards the north-west and close

[1] Linschoten, II, 141.

to a large town called Nichabourg [Nīshāpūr]; the other, which is called "the new", is five days' journey from it. These stones from the new are of an inferior blue, tending to white, and are little esteemed, and one may purchase as many of them as he likes at small cost. But for many years the King of Persia has prohibited mining in "the old rock" for anyone but himself, because there are no gold workers in the country except those who work in thread, who are ignorant of the art of enamelling on gold, and without knowledge of design and engraving, and he uses for the decoration of swords, daggers, and other work, instead of enamel, these turquoises of "the old rock" which are cut and arranged in patterns like flowers and other figures which the jewellers make. This catches the eye and passes as a laborious work, but it is wanting in design' (Tavernier, II, 81).

LOADSTONE OR MAGNETITE

Although Sir Thomas Roe categorically asserts that there are no loadstones in India (p. 91, bottom), Linschoten assures us that it is found in great quantity and in many places in India. 'The Indians say, that if a man use dayly to eate a little of that stone, it preserveth him and maketh him look yong, and that he shall never looke olde: wherefore the Kinges and great Lordes of India use it in pottes and vesselles, therein to [eate and] seeth their meate, thereby as they beleeve to preserve their youthes' (Linschoten, II, 142).

BLOODSTONE

In an inventory of the Old Joint Stock on p. 61 of *E. F. I.* 1618-1621 we have 119 *maḥmūdīs* as the price of 8,500 bloodstones.

CORAL

'Although coral does not rank among precious stones in Europe,' remarks Tavernier, 'it is nevertheless held in high esteem in the other quarters of the globe, and it is one of the most beautiful of nature's productions, so that there are some nations who prefer it to precious stones' (II, 104). The Japanese, who esteem neither pearls nor precious stones, value beautiful beads of coral. The Portuguese, who formerly did a large trade in Japan, could obtain for a coral as much as 20,000 écus or £4,500. 'The common people wear it and use it as an ornament for the neck and arms throughout Asia, but principally towards the north in the territories of the Great Mogul, and beyond them, in the mountains, of the Kingdoms of Assam and Bhutān' (*Ibid.*, II, 106-7).

Coral came chiefly from the Red Sea and the Mediterranean.[1]

The run of prices, the quality of the articles and the conditions of demand and supply in India may be gathered from scattered notices in the *E.F.I.* and *Letters Received*.

The best market for polished coral was Surat.[2] But as regards actual consumption, while great quantities of coral beads were absorbed by Bengal,[3] the Deccan was the greatest buyer of red coral, which was much

[1] *E.F.I.* 1618-1621, p. 131 and *E.F.I.* 1624-1629, p. XXXV.

[2] *E.F.I.* 1618-1621, p. 326.

[3] *Ibid.*, p. 259.

worn by the people and buried with them when they died.[1]

The superior coral known as the "Grezio" or "Gretzo" was in great request.[2] We are also told that coral in round or long beads and branches sold best;[3] likewise coral of deepest colour and in thickest pieces, though short.[4]

Between 1622 and 1648 the price of good coral was 9 to 10 rupees a seer (of ¾ lb.);[5] and in the years 1665-1668 it ranged between 10 and 16 rupees per seer.[6] Coarse coral was, however, available at all prices from ¾ of a rupee to about 7 rupees a seer.[7]

---

[1] *Letters Received*, I, 307.

[2] *E.F.I.* 1642-1645, p. 174.

[3] *Letters Received*, III, 10.

[4] *E.F.I.* 1618-1621, p. 326.

[5] *E.F.I.* 1622-1623, p. 8; *E. F.I.* 1634-1636, p. 24; *E.F.I.* 1637-1641, p. 204; *E.F.I.* 1642-1645, p. 210.

[6] *E.F.I.* 1665-1667, p. 31; *E.F.I.* 1668-1669, p. 3.

[7] *E.F.I.* 1630-1633, p. 31; and 84. *E.F.I.* 1634-1636, p. 23; and 69. *E.F.I.* 1642-1645, p. 210; *E.F.I.* 1665-1667, p. 31; *E.F.I.* 1668-1669, p. 3.

Prices of coral beads in Bengal ran as follows :—

Beads of	12	beads to a *tānk*	at	6	*tānks*	for a rupee
,,	6	,,	,,	2	,,	,, ,, ,,
,,	4	,,	,,	1¾	,,	,, ,, ,,
,,	3	,,	,,	1½	,,	,, ,, ,,

(*E.F.I.* 1618-1621, p. 259).

Enclosing a copy of the custom-house valuation of the coral, the factors write to the Company, ' By this it will be seen that the sort called " recaduti " of 8*s*. or 9*s*. the lb., yields most benefit ; the small sort now sent, called " tiraglia brutura," is not so much in demand. A hundred chests of coral will sell yearly, *viz*., fifty of from 2*s*. to 8*s*. the lb. and fifty of from 8*s*. to 15*s*.' (*E.F.I*. 1630-1633, p. 31). We are informed in a footnote that 'recaduti ' means ' dead coral, ' and that 'tiraglia brutura ' signifies the rough growths and crusts that form on the plant.

A fine ornament of coral which Ṣafi Khān meant to present to Jahāñgir on his birthday is thus described in *E.F.I*. 1622-1623 : ' The principall thinge in her [the junk belonging to

Ṣafī Khān, the Governor of Cambay] is a tree currall sett in gould by artt, made to distill watter from the topp unseene, rounde aboutt the branches. Itt is contayned in five chestes, and beinge by us vallued itt was thought to bee worth 2,000*l*., itt beinge procured by the Governor of Cambaya to bee made in Goa against the beirthdaye of the Greatte Mogull and to him to bee presented, for which intentt this juncke was purposely sentt' (P. 215).

We learn incidentally that the charge for polishing coral at a place in the Bījāpur kingdom was 10 pagodas, *i.e.*, about 40 rupees, a *man*.[1]

LAPIS LAZULI

Lapis Lazuli, says Goodchild, 'has been known from very remote times, being much used by the Egyptians, and to a lesser extent by the Assyrians. Epiphanius, Bishop of Salamis, says the Tables of the Law given to Moses were inscribed on Lapis Lazuli. The Romans used it to some extent as a material for engraving on' (P. 240).

---

[1] *E.F.I*, 1618-1621, p. 265.

'It is cut as a flat plaque, or *en cabochon*; more often it is worked into vases and other small ornamental objects, though now the solid material is not so often used as thin slices, which are veneered on. It is largely used, too, for mosaics and in the ornamentation of luxurious buildings such as the palaces of the Russian Czars. Formerly it was the sole source of the beautiful pigment ultramarine, which was greatly esteemed on account of the purity of its colour and permanence. Now, however, the pigment is made artificially, though the artificial product does not command nearly the same price' (*Ibid.*, 242-43). The columns of St. Isaac's Cathedral at Petrograd present a fine example of the use of lapis lazuli for architectural decoration.

Clavijo, writing in Tīmūr's time, speaks of 'the city of Aquivi, which is in the country where the lapis lazuli comes from :......... This city of Aquivi is......ten days' journey in the direction of India the Less, but it lies rather to the southward of Badakhshān.'[1] The

[1] *Embassy to Tamerlane*, 274. For the whole of this quotation see pp. 262-64 above.

translator, however, cannot trace the place on the modern maps.[1]

The lapis lazuli mine in Badakhshān (Afghānistān) is mentioned by Tavernier and Marco Polo.

On 21 *Zū'l-qa'd*, 1044, the envoy of Nazr Muḥammad Khān, ruler of Balkh, presented to Shāh Jahān, on behalf of his master, 100 horses, 50 camels, male and female, 100 maunds of lapis lazuli, some brocades of Tūrān, sables, carpets, rugs, Russia leather, some pieces of porcelain, etc.—total price, Rs. 70,000.[2]

Soon after Aurangzeb had brought the war of succession to a successful issue, says Bernier, the ambassadors of the Khāns of Balkh and Samarkand waited on the Emperor, ostensibly to offer congratulations, really to conciliate his good will. Among the presents they brought were some boxes of lapis lazuli[3] (Bernier, 118). The translator adds under

[1] *Ibid.*, p. 360.

[2] *B.N.*, I, ii, 89 ; *A. S.*, II, 99-100.

[3] Manucci also refers to this present (*Storia*, II, 37).

this text: 'Lapis-lazuli was largely used in the pietra dura work in the Táj; and these Tartar ambassadors may have been bringing some of it as a tribute or offering to the Mogul Court for this very purpose. This tomb, although finished in 1648 as far as the mere structure is concerned, was probably worked at for many years afterwards (' built by Titans, finished by jewellers'), as much of the exquisite detail of its decorations could not have been carried out in any other way' (p. 118, f. n. 1). This suggestion, I am afraid, is unacceptable. In the first place the Tāj was completed not in 1648 A.C., but towards the end of 1052 A.H., which corresponds to January-February, 1643 A.C. Secondly, when we are told definitely by 'Abdu'l-Hamīd that the mausoleum took nearly twelve years to build, and was finally completed, at the total cost of 50 lakhs of rupees, about *Z̲ū'l-qa'd,* 1052,[1] we have no justification whatever for supposing that the finishing and decoration of the tomb straggled on till early in Aurangzeb's time, *i.e.*, for another eighteen years. It is much more reason-

[1] *B. N.*, II, 330.

able to assume that the earlier consignment of 100 maunds of this mineral, which was presented to Shāh Jahān (mentioned in the last paragraph) was used in the pietra dura work in the Tāj. In fact it must have come quite handy for use, and may actually have been sent for the express purpose of being used by the builders of the famous monument, the renown of which must have travelled beyond the Indian frontiers.

MOTHER-OF-PEARL

This is the substance which lines the interior of many species of molluscs, and is similar in nature to the pearl (*Enc. Brit.*, XV, 852). It is cut out and used extensively for such purposes as making buttons, handles of cutlery, etc. It is also used in the inlaying of Japanese and Chinese lacquers, European lacquered papier-mâché work, and trays, etc., and as an ornamental inlay generally (*Ibid.*, XVII, 422).

'Its beautiful iridescence and lustre are due to that well-known optical phenomenon, the interference of light' (*Ibid.*, XV, 852).

About the mother-of-pearl Linschoten has the following :—

The Indians know how to prepare and clean it. ' They bring many of them into Portingale to serve for to drinke in, and to keepe for an ornament, [and for pleasure] specially those that come out of China and Bengalen, some guilt and painted with colours [very faire some] wrought with branches and other figures, as we dayly see them brought thether [Orig. Dutch : 'hither']. In India they make divers thinges of them, as deskes, tables, cubbards, tables to play on [backgammon boards], boxes, staves for women to beare in their hands, and a thousand such fine devises, which are all inlaid and covered with this Chanco or Mother of Pearle, very faire to beholde, and very workmanlike made, and are in India so common that there is almost no place in those countries but they have of them. It is likewise much caried abroad, both into Portingale, and els where, but they are most used in India, for there the women, speciallie those of Bengala use to weare manillias, or bracelets of them about their armes, that is to say, those of most account, and they must not take a maidens maidenhead from her that is of any estate or degree, but she must have some of these mother of Pearle bracelets about her armes, which at this day is yet much used, [and observed,] whereby it is verie much worne' (II, 135-36).

Linschoten is apparently confusing mother-of-pearl with ivory in the latter part of this passage.

Perhaps the finest specimen in India of mother-of-pearl inlay on a large scale is the canopy of the mausoleum of Ḥaẓrat Salīm Chishtī at Fatḥpur Sīkrī, which is thus described by E. W. Smith:

'Salîm's cenotaph is of white marble surmounted by a wooden canopy inlaid with mother-of-pearl tesseræ..............

The outside of the canopy is entirely encrusted with mother-of-pearl, laid in geometrical designs, bound at the corners and sides with copper. The cornice is worked with the favourite fish-scale ornament so common to the period in which the mausoleum was built.

Running through it is an embattlemented pattern in ebony, which material is also freely used upon the four-armed bracket capitals the sub-caps and the bases of the columns. The capitals and brackets are very intricately and delicately carved, and, in order to protect the fine inlaying upon them, the *arrises* of the mouldings are bound with copper. To show clearly the nature of the inlaying, a portion of the eaves around the top of the canopy has been omitted on the drawing. The brackets project up two tiers and beneath each is a circular pendant, tipped with copper; across the centre of the lower of the two brackets is a band of copper and one of ebony inlaid with quatrefoils in mother-of-pearl. The combination of the mother-of-pearl and ebony is very pleasing. The full effect of the treatment is seen upon the bases of the columns one of which is illustrated on Plate XLII. As it is impossible to reproduce the peculiar nacrous sheen of the mother-of-pearl upon a drawing, it has been shown in white upon the illustration ; whilst the ebony is in black.

The same design, or nearly the same, appears

on each of the bases, but that upon one side of the base is unlike that on the other. The inlaying is so intricate that it looks like damask-work, but in mother-of-pearl instead of gold or copper wire. Each little piece of mother-of-pearl is exactly shaped and fitted into the allotted position previously prepared for it, and then secured with minute brass pins and shellac. The minute strips of ebony between each piece of mother-of-pearl are secured in like manner and are perfectly flush with the face of the mother-of-pearl. It is impossible to describe the effect of the mother-of-pearl as seen in the dim light of the mortuary chamber. It is one of those things which defy description, and in order to realize its beauty it must be seen. The inlaying is most minutely and beautifully executed. There is nothing like it elsewhere in Northern India, and it is very doubtful whether such an elegant piece of like workmanship exists in any other part of India' (E. W. Smith, *The Moghul Architecture of Fathpur-Sikri*, Pt. III, 21-22).

CHINESE PORCELAIN

Porcelain is an important subject. Not

only is it interesting in itself, but we know that the Imperial Treasury contained some 25 lakhs' worth of 'most elegant vessels of every kind in porcelain and coloured glass.' We are, I think, justified in according it a more extended treatment than to the majority of other articles.

In the passages selected here we have been at pains to avoid specialized treatment and technical terminology. It is hoped the reader, who requires an introduction to the subject, will find the following smooth and interesting reading :—

'Every connoisseur and every unprejudiced potter,' says Mr. Burton in his monograph on Porcelain, 'will admit, in his lucid moments that the porcelain of the Chinese marks the very crowning point of the potter's achievements. We may single out the glazed work of the ancient Egyptians or Assyrians, the painted terra-cotta vases of the Greeks, the brilliantly-enamelled faïence of the Persians, or the majolica of the Italians, as worthy of our high regard, yet Chinese porcelain surpasses all these as much in sheer beauty of colour as in technical skill and in the wide range of its accomplishment' (46).

'The idea that a cup of porcelain changed colour and flew into pieces directly a poisonous draught was poured into it, was implicitly believed for many centuries. This belief was current not only in Europe but in Persia, India, and other Asiatic countries where porcelain was not made, so that we should probably be justified in regarding these false notions as the fables invented by cunning dealers, whether Chinese or Arab, anxious to enhance the value of their wares' (*Ibid.*, 47).

The chinaware in favour in the better Mughul days was chiefly that of the Ming period (1368-1644), though there may also have been pieces of the time of the Sung dynasty (960-1259). So in the account that follows we shall confine ourselves to the history and characteristics of the porcelain of the Ming period.

The famous chinaware of the Ming period (1368-1644) was manufactured in the imperial factory at Ching-tê Chên, near the Po-yang lake in Kiangse, rendered famous throughout the world by the fine white porcelain made there. 'As this ware lent itself peculiarly well to painted decoration,' says the *Enc. Brit.* article, 'the vogue for painted porcelain rapidly replaced the old Sung taste for monochromes' (*Enc. Brit.*, XVIII, p. 366).

Hitherto, says Mr. Burton, 'all the colour effects were in the nature of coloured glazes applied either on plain shapes or on vessels that had previously been decorated with incised or embossed ornament. The first new departure, and a most natural one, was to decorate the piece with ornamental schemes, either of conventional foliage or of figure subjects, in which the different patterns of the design, isolated by raised lines, could be filled in with different glazes so as to produce an effect roughly analogous to that of a design in cloisonné enamel' (W. Burton, *Porcelain*, 66).

'With the discovery and the extended use of the materials of true porcelain, *kao-lin* and *pe-tun-tse*, the possibility must soon have presented itself to the delighted potter of preparing an absolutely white translucent porcelain, and when once this possibility had been realised there can be no doubt that everything else would give way before it..............We read at an early period of pure white porcelain made of the utmost thinness and delicacy, so that its translucence might be most apparent, and decorated only with delicate patterns, generally of dragons, waves or clouds, sharply engraved with a steel point in the dry clay before it was glazed and fired. Ware of this kind is said to have been produced at the famous factory of Ting-chou early in the twelfth century of our era. Occasionally the same ware was produced with a bright purple glaze having a tint like that of ripe grapes, and more rarely still with a beautiful clear black glaze. Dr. Bushell has translated a description of some of these early pieces left by a Chinese connoisseur of the sixteenth century, who, in describing a duck-headed vase of this Ting-chou porcelain, says: "I have seen hundreds of specimens of the white, scores of the purple-brown, but only this one of black in all my life"' (*Porcelain*, 67-68).

'The Chinese esteem most highly the blue-and-white of the Hsüan-tê period (1426-1435), and of the period Ch'êng-hua (1465-1487), while they relegate to the third place the blue-and-white produced during the reign of Yung-lo (1403-1424)' (*Ibid.*, 68).

The cobalt used during these reigns is known as the Mohammedan blue, probably obtained from Baluchistan, where deposits of the purest cobalt ore, a mineral sometimes called cobalt bloom, has been found, which might be used without any other preparation than that of grinding and levigation.

Supply of the Mohammedan blue failed in the latter part of the fifteenth century, when the Chinese potter had to fall back upon his native ore. With this the character of the blue colour at once deteriorated. During the Chêng-tê period (1506-21), however, further supplies of the Mohammedan blue were arranged for at a cost of twice its weight in gold; and at this exorbitant price it remained available down to the middle of the sixteenth century. After this date the Chinese had to depend again on the cobalt pigment prepared by many refinings of their native ore. It must be said that nothing ever equalled in brilliance the Mohammedan blue, which is often spoken of as rivalling the blue of the sapphire (*Ibid.*, 68-69).

Again, an underglaze red, made from copper, was used by the Chinese at a very early date. When we remember how difficult it has proved, even for the most expert of modern scientific potters, to produce this underglaze red colour, we bow before the Chinese in respect and admiration (*Ibid.*, 69). 'This magnificent underglaze red appears to have been obtained in its utmost perfection during the early part of the Ming dynasty, for we find it especially mentioned in the Hsüan-tê period (1426-1435)' (70).

The wonderful eggshell porcelain pieces, which the Chinese called "Bodyless," first appeared during the early times of the Ming dynasty. 'The true eggshell porcelain must always have required the utmost skill and dexterity of manipulation, for its substance has been reduced to so thin a layer that in a fine specimen it almost seems as if there could be no clay left between the two layers of glaze. At all events, from the Yung-lo period (1403-1424) eggshell porcelains of varying degrees of delicacy, attesting the skill of different generations of potters, have been made practically without interruption. In spite of the extreme thinness of such pieces, the finest specimens had elaborate designs engraved, with a steel tool, in the paste before firing. The designs generally take the form of dragons in the midst of clouds or waves, the whole work being executed with such delicacy and precision as to leave us absolutely amazed at the audacity which could conceive, and the patient skill which could execute such marvels of technique. The finest early eggshell pieces, covered with incised patterns of this nature, were generally in pure white; so that the design is barely visible unless the vessel be held against the light or filled with a liquid. Considering that the difficulties of manufacturing such pieces must always have been formidable, it was only natural that a similar style of incised or engraved decoration should have been used on vessels of ordinary thickness, and these were often covered with delicately coloured glazes, of which a beautiful pale-yellow seems to have been most highly prized, especially in the Hung-Chih period (1488-1505), and the Chèngtê period (1506-1521).

At the same early date, too, another delicate and difficult method of decorating white porcelain was invented. This is the decoration so often known among modern collectors as "grain of rice" pattern, where the design is actually cut out of the vessel while it is yet in the clay state, and then, when the glaze-coating is applied, the glaze fills up the perforations, which become like so many window-openings in the piece. This particularly charming method of decoration, which was also adopted by the Persian potters for their transparent ware, has excited the greatest interest among modern European porcelain-makers' (P. 71-72).

Some European manufacturers have in the nineteenth century made creditable attempts to imitate that kind of ware, but, in justice to the Chinese potter, it must be admitted that 'they can never rank for subtle beauty and delicacy with the dainty white Chinese pieces' (72).

Towards the close of the Ming dynasty the Chinese use of on-glaze colours in the decoration of porcelain comes in, thus foreshadowing the course which the decoration of pottery has practically taken in all the great pottery-centres of the world. This new manner of working, *i.e.*, painting on the fired glaze, 'replaces the freedom and abandon as well as the rich depths of colour of the earlier work by finer, more delicately drawn, more precise, and, as an artist would say, " tighter " work, inevitable from the changed technical method ' (72).

CHINAWARE IN MUGHUL INDIA

The Imperial Treasury, as we have said, had huge stores of Chinese porcelain of the most valuable kind ; and in contemporary paintings we see chinaware of the Ming period reposing in niches in Mughul interiors. So we notice that China was used not only cn the table but also for purely decorative purposes.

There must have been, among the rest, a considerable amount of the willow-green porcelain known as Celadon, which has been so popular among Muslim countries throughout the ages as actually to suggest a Muslim origin. This last view, however, is discredited by modern authorities, who hold that the old celadon, which must be regarded as one of the earliest forms of porcelain, originated in China (Burton, *Porcelain*, 64).

Colonel T. H. Hendley has the following on celadon ware in India: 'In old Mogul towns in India, until lately, a good many specimens of celadon plates or vases might be purchased. It is said that this ware was in great demand even so far back as the Sung Dynasty—that is, from the tenth to the thirteenth centuries. The want was most largely met with, however, in the days of the East India Company, by importation from China. It was thought that it possessed in common with rhinoceros horn, the quality of splitting or breaking when brought into contact with poisoned food; hence the value attributed to it by Mohammedans, and especially by the Moguls. Dr. Bushell informs us that the presence of poison was said to be revealed by the exudation of a white humour from the cup or from the surface of a rod of rhinoceros horn put into the liquid to test it.

The belief was prevalent from very early times in China and Sumatra. The ware is extremely heavy. The basis is red and the glaze, which is very thick, has a dark willow-green colour. The vases are generally crackled, and the plates or dishes are deep and sometimes have fluted or gadrooned edges. Beneath the glaze there are usually bouquets of flowers (generally chrysanthemums), fishes and other designs................................

....

.........The bright grass-green celadons of the Sung Dynasty (960-1280 A. D.) are certainly rare in India, but the greyish-green or sea-green of later dynasties, as the old Lung Ch'uan of the Ming period (1368-1644), which Dr.Bushell says are quite in the style of the antecedent Sung Dynasty, are common. Some of the dishes purchased at Delhi thirty years ago, of which one is illustrated (Plate 2), are exactly like that shewn in Plate II, Vol. II of his work, though they are generally more worn. As the Sung productions vary from pale sea-green to deep olive, and those of later periods are also of the latter colour, it is not easy to distinguish them, especially as both may exhibit plain and crackled surfaces. Most of the Delhi specimens are dark grey-green and crackled. The glaze is generally very thick and runs down at the foot or border. The paste is usually red or brown, and is very hard. The popular Mogul or Delhi name was Ghori ware' ("Foreign Industrial Art Products imported into India" in *The Journal of Indian Art and Industry*, No. 129, for Jan., 1915).

We are not prepared to endorse the view that the *ghoris*, as they are known in India, are all celadon ware.

Clavijo tells us that Tīmūr carried away from Damascus, among other artisans, 'craftsmen in glass and porcelain, who are known to be the best in all the world. From Turkey he had brought their gun-smiths who make the arquebus, and all men of other crafts wheresoever he found them, such as the silver-smiths and the masons.'[1]

'On Thursday, the 22nd [*Sha'bān*, 1016 *A.H.*],' says Jahāngīr, 'on the invitation of Āṣaf Khān, I went with my ladies to his house and passed the

[1] *Embassy to Tamerlane*, 288.

night there. The next day he presented before me his own offerings, of the value of ten lacs of rupees, in jewels and jewelled things, robes, elephants, and horses. Some single rubies and jacinths and some pearls, also silk cloths with some pieces of porcelain from China and Tartary, were accepted, and I made a present of the rest to him.'[1] The words in the text are *Faghfūrī* and *Khaṭā'ī* porcelain. The china of Faghfūr (according to Steingass, a place in China celebrated for its porcelain) and that of Khaṭā (*i.e.*, North China) would thus seem to be different kinds of ware, specifically named according to their provenance. This is corroborated by the entries that follow.

On VII New Year's Day the presents sent by Khān Daurān were placed before Jahāṅgīr. They included 45 horses, two strings of camels, porcelain of Khaṭā (or Northern China), fur-coats[2] of sable and other rarities of Kābul and its neighbourhood.[3]

---

[1] *Tūzuk*, 63; R. & B., I, 132.

[2] This is correct, if the reading *postīnhā* be accepted. Some MSS. have *posthā*. In that case the meaning would be 'skins of sable.'

[3] *Tūzuk*, 100; R. & B., I, 206.

In the records of X R. Y. we have the presentation by Lashkar Khān of three strings of Persian camels, twenty cups and plates of *Khaṭā'ī* porcelain, and twenty greyhounds.[1]

Under date 5 *Urdībihisht*, XI R. Y., Jahāṅgīr writes as follows : 'On the 5th (Urdībihisht) 30 Iraq and Turki horses that Murtaẓā Khān had sent from Lahore were brought before me, as also 63 horses, 15 camels, male and female, a bundle of crane's (*kulang*) plumes,[2] 9 '*āqirī* (?),[3] 9 veined fish-teeth, 9 pieces of china from Tartary [*Khaṭā'ī*], 3 guns, etc., from Khān Daurān, which he had sent from Kabul, were accepted.'[4]

---

[1] *Tūzuk*, 143.

[2] Is not 'a bundle of plumes for the aigrette' a better translation? The translators apparently read the word *kulangī* instead of *kalgī*, which latter is found both in the printed texts and the P. U. L. MS.

[3] The word '*āqirī* is correct, as it is found in all MSS. The translators' note on this passage (p. 452) is on the right track. '*Āqirī* is connected with '*uqār*, which is a bird whose feathers are used for aigrettes (*Bahār-i-'Ajam* and Steingass)—perhaps a heron.

[4] *Tūzuk*, 158; R. & B., I, 322-23.

Faghfūrī porcelain is also mentioned in *Qawā'id-i-Saḥanat-i-Shāh Jahān* (P. U. L. MS., f. 21*b*).

Some pieces of porcelain, sent by Nazr Muḥammad Khān of Balkh have already been mentioned under Lapis lazuli.[1]

Among the events of the year 1094 we read in *Ma'āsir-i-'Ālamgīrī* that on the death of Ḥāfiz Muḥammad Amīn Khān, governor of Ahmadābād, his possessions were brought to court. They included, besides cash and animals, ten cases of porcelain of all kinds (P. 226).

On Pl. XIX (*a*) of *L.E.A.* we find two china dishes, one (No. A. 368) blue and white China Dish, said to have belonged to Mīrzā Jahāṅgīr, s/o Akbar II, the other (No. A. 369) blue and white China Dish, said to have belonged to Akbar II.

European notices can be taken up now:

Sir Thomas Roe assures us that chinaware was in great request in India.[2]

---

[1] See p. 397 above.

[2] Roe, 445 and 459 (bottom).

He tells the East India Company in one place that 'faire China bedsteeds' would be rich presents at the Mughul court (P. 99).

We have already seen (under Rock-crystal) that the King of Bisampore's ambassador brought to Jahāngīr's court, among other very valuable things, 'China wares and one figure of christall, which the King accepted more then that masse of wealth' (Roe, 99).

Roe, it appears, wante, when going home, to buy some china to take home with him. In a letter to Nicholas Bangham dated April 1, 1617, he says: 'I heare yow have fine and curious China ware. If you will spare me some dozen fine cupps and dishes (such as yow will choose), I will give as much as any man. All these I desier yow will keepe for mee till wee meete; for I hope to pass downe by Brampoor toward England in October, and I would not trouble yow soe much but that I am resolved homward, and would willingly carry somewhat. My stock will not reach to things of profitt and trade; therefore, seeing I shall not gett riches, I would yet pleasure my frends'

(P. 360). So he wanted these for presentation at home.

Bangham apparently bought only two cups for him, and those dearly ; for, says Roe, in a letter to Bangham written three months later, 'I thancke yow for the two China cupps, and doe extreamely like them for the curiositye. Their price I must bee content with, because the buyer cannot make yt ; but they are dearer here at that rate by much then in England. I doe not desiere any more of that sort so small ; but if yow can fitt mee out of the rest with a parcell of fine dishes or cupps for use, or any peece, as a bottle or eywer, and of the best sorts......to make up this summe 100 or 80 *rup.*, I desier yow to make your choyce for mee' (P. 367).

It appears that the cups bought by Bangham were for ornamental purposes, while Roe wanted some china for use. Still Roe appreciates the beauty of the articles bought. One of these two cups, we are informed in another place, cost eight rupees (p. 400, f.n. 1). We thus learn incidentally that Roe desired to get a dozen cups and dishes for 80 or 100 rupees, but could not.

On October 12, 1617, Roe saw Prince Shāh Jahān in his private room, where Āṣaf Khān had taken him, and presented him with 'a small China gold-chaine, in a China cup' (P. 400). This was one of the two cups Bangham had bought for the ambassador.

Under January 13, 1618, we have the following entry in Roe's diary: 'The Dutch came to court with a great present of China ware, sanders [*i.e.*, sandalwood], parrots and cloaves' (P. 427). This is supported by other reports to the effect that the Dutch were strong in the porcelain trade.[1]

Hawkins narrates the story of a 'faire China dish (which cost ninetie Rupias, or fortie five Rials of eight)' belonging to Jagāṅgīr, which was broken by a mischance, when the Emperor was out in camp. The officer in charge, 'knowing how deerely the King loved this dish above the rest,' sent a trusty servant to 'China-

[1] See below.

machina '[1] over land, hoping that the dish would come before the Emperor remembered it. After a lapse of two years, before the new dish had arrived, the Emperor thought of the old one. When told that the dish was broken, he very nearly flogged the life out of the nobleman, and was sending him to prison for life when, on the intercession of a prince, he was ordered not to come before him till he had procured a similar dish. The Emperor advanced him five thousand rupees towards his expenses of a journey to China, and a quarter of his *jāgīr* was restored to him. Hawkins says that he had been fourteen months travelling, and had not yet come back; but the King of Persia, it so happened, had a like dish, and on hearing this pitiful tale, had sent it to the officer, who, at the time of Hawkins' departure, was going home (Purchas, III, 39-40).

[1] Māchīn, a popular corruption of Mahāchīn, is a very old Hindu name. It means Great China, and was vaguely used for the Chinese empire.

With Persian writers Mahāchīn, strictly, is South China while Khaṭā (English, Cathay) is North China; but Chīn Māchīn is often used in the vague sense of China. And that is how it is used here.

The E.I. Company had no porcelain trade in India worth speaking of. Consequently very little information about this trade in India is available in the E. I. Company's correspondence (*E.F.I.* and *Letters*). From the constant complaints of the factors that the china is bad and 'crazed' and broken and unvendible,[1] we are led to infer that their packing was careless and their buying defective. On their own showing the Dutch enjoyed a prosperous trade in this commodity. We are told that, 'at present all their estate [at Masulipatam] is in chinaware, "which is as britle as their harts to us are fickle."'[2] Again, 'the Chinaware which either Cartwright or Clark took in exchange for lead will not sell for a tenth of what it is rated at. No more should be sent, for the Dutch supply this place [Masulipatam] at such cheap rates that it does not pay to bring such brittle ware.'[3]

---

[1] *E.F.I.* 1618-1621, pp. 47, 203 and 263;
E.F.I. 1624-1629, pp. 281, 284 and 297;
E.F.I. 1637-1641, pp. 256 and 266.
Also *E.F.I.* 1642-1645, p. 284, which, however, is written from Basra.

[2] *E.F.I.* 1637-1641, p. 45.

[3] *Ibid.*, p. 190. Also see *Ibid.*, p. 241.

As for prices, the following quotation gives the cost price of each of the articles mentioned, at Bantam (in Java) :—'From a note on the latter [the cargo list] we find that of the porcelain the prime cost was : saucer dishes, nearly 2*d*. apiece: flat sallet [salad] dishes, about 3½*d*.; sallet cups, 3½*d*.; posset dishes, 4*d*.; small ("quarter") basins, 1*s*. 9*d*.; larger ("half") basins, 2*s*. 6*d*.; largest ("whole") basins, 5*s*.' (*Letters*, III, 324-25).

From the low run of prices detailed here, we gather that the E.I. Co. did not go in for higher lines in the porcelain business. No wonder that they derived small profit and lost heart.

The following is part of a letter, dated May 15, 1617, and written by the factors at Ispahan to Bantam. The requirements appertain no doubt to the Persian Court, but the social customs and domestic conditions in the two countries were so similar that we may presume the requisitions to apply quite as much to India as to the country to which it owed its civilization and culture: 'I have been entreated by the King's treasurer and favourite to procure him divers necessaries and toys for the King's use, according to a remembrance he hath given me. Part of them being what Suratt and India can furnish, I have to them written for. These hereunder specified in your Southern parts are only to be found; pleasing you to order their sending accordingly:

Cheney [China] dishes in sorts, 200 pieces to serve meat at table. Their dishes here are like our English, broad and not deep, and such ones he desireth.

Cheney dishes, 50 pieces of the largest and fairest can be gotten of the same making. These are intended when the King feasteth.

6 basins and ewers of Cheney.

100 small coffa dishes [coffee cups].

....

We give you to understand that Cheney ware of all sorts is here a good commodity, being much in request; but we doubt in no great quantity. Besides, the brittleness of the commodity is considerable' (*Letters*, V, 246).

'In obedience to instructions from Sir Thomas Chamberlain to purchase rarities for presentation to King Charles, Buckeridge bought twelve China dishes : "a sort reported to breake if any poyson bee put into them, but I dare not affirme that as a truth " ' (*E.F.I.* 1661-1664, p. 392).

IVORY

A term properly confined to the material which forms the tusk of the elephant, and, for commercial purposes, almost entirely to that of the male elephant, but often extended to a similar substance obtained from the walrus, hippopotamus, narwhal, cachalot or sperm-whale, etc., although only the first two of these are really important.

ELEPHANT IVORY

These tusks are sometimes of tremendous size, a single specimen occasionally weighing 200 ℔. ' The ivory from the African elephants is the most esteemed on account of its superior density and whiteness, but a certain amount is also obtained from India, Ceylon, Burma, and the islands of the Eastern Archipelago. In African elephants both the males and females have tusks, although those of the males are larger, but in the Indian species the females are practically tuskless' (*Everyman's Encyclopaedia*, VII, 718).

The quality of ivory varies according to the districts whence it is obtained , the soft variety of the eastern parts of Africa being the most esteemed.

The price varies with size and soundness of the tusks, ranging from £10 to £90 per cwt.

Special qualities of ivory, which have been recognized from the earliest times, are its beautiful texture, and tints, its perfect elasticity and adaptability to the carver's tools.

As for modern industrial application, ivory is used at present in the manufacture of billiard-balls, cutlery handles, piano-keys, brushware and toilet articles, chessmen, carved figures, and other useful and ornamental articles.

Ivory carving is a highly interesting art. 'Since earliest times ivory has been used either alone or in conjunction with silver and bronze as a decorative material, and it has been both carved and engraved. Ivory has always been used considerably for the decoration of palaces, and the Romans sent an ivory throne to Porsena, while, in the nineteenth century, an Indian Prince sent one to Queen Victoria. Ivory has also been used a great deal for religious purposes in such things as crucifixes, the heads of pastoral staves, liturgical combs, and even altar-pieces. Secular works of art, in which ivory has been employed, include seals, hunting horns, knick-knacks, snuff-boxes, toilet combs, mirror cases, chessmen, and draughts. Prehistoric man used pieces of bone, horn, and ivory for his sketch-book, and scratched on it drawings of animals The ancient Egyptians and Assyrians used ivory for domestic purposes and for the decoration of furniture but Egyptian ivory statuettes have also been found. The Greeks used ivory for the decorations on the trappings of their horses and for the bosses of their shields and for small boxes and caskets, but we possess few examples of Greek ivories, especially of the early period. Of Roman ivories we have a great number of consular diptychs, often from writing tablets and plaques which are beautifully carved in relief. The subjects of these carvings were usually classical myths or pictures of Roman gods. The earliest Christian ivories in existence date from the time of Constantine and among these we have pyxes carved from ivory tusks, plaques, and book-covers. Byzantine ivories are very numerous and beautiful, and if the figure of Christ, so often portrayed, is inclined to be stereotyped, the decorative designs of these ivories are excellent. Up to the end of the fourteenth century, ivory carvings were usually of religious subjects, although often used for secular purposes, but after this date hunting scenes, deeds of chivalry, and pictures of tournaments were depicted, the sculptures being influenced by the romantic literature of the period. In India, ivory has been much used for caskets, many of which are extremely beautiful and elaborate. Chinese ivories are often more clever than beautiful, and consist chiefly of elaborately carved balls and models of villas; in the latter, however, some very beautiful work is to be found. Japanese ivories are usually very small, but very well designed and finished. Most Japanese ivories are comparatively modern, and the Japanese have used ivory a great deal for "netsukes," which are a kind of toggle used in connection with their smoking gear. In modern times ivory has been used for sculpture, either alone or in conjunction with bronze and jewels. One modern example of ivory sculpture that may be mentioned is the "Lama" by George Frampton. This piece is the bust of a woman. The face is life-size and carved out of ivory, while the headdress and dress are of bronze (*Ibid.*, pp. 718-20).

The ivory throne sent by the Indian Prince to Queen Victoria (referred to in this passage) is a little more fully described in the following quotation from a monograph[1] published by the Government of India in 1883:

'Some will no doubt remember the ivory throne and footstool exhibited in 1851, the gift of the Raja of Travancore to Her Majesty the Queen. It is a remarkable specimen of carved ivory, displaying skill in the design and execution. The ornament of the back and sides is very elaborate, and consists of bands and compartments of conventional foliage, human figures

---

[1] *Fifty-one Photographic Illustrations taken by order of the Government of India of some selected objects shown at the Third Exhibition of Native Fine and Industrial Art opened at Simla by His Excellency the Viceroy on the 24th September, 1881. London*, 1883.

and animals, the style and arrangement of which derives its character from the carved architectural ornament of Dravidian art' (P. 5).

The rest of the note on Carved Ivory is not devoid of interest: 'India has always been famed for ivory carvings, which are applied to furniture and to all descriptions of useful and ornamental objects. The modern work is produced mostly at Murshedabad in Bengal, and at Shahpur, Amritsar and Delhi in the Punjab, at Bhurtpur, Jodhpur and Udaipur in Rajputana, in Bombay, in Assam, and in Burma, and at Vizagapatam and Travancore in Madras. Small statuettes, models of elephants and other animals, carved paper-cutters, chowris or fly whisks, sword and knife handles, chess-boards and chessmen, tankards, combs, and all descriptions of boxes, are among the most commonly produced articles. Carving in ivory produced in India is done for the most part by hand, and is much to be admired for elaboration of detail and for picturesque grouping of figures and animals. The geometrical and foliated ornament is always first-rate, and the production of carved ivory suitable for the application to furniture and to useful objects should be developed and encouraged' (*Ibid.*).

IVORY AND IVORY WORK IN INDIA

Now we can jot down some bits of information about ivory and articles of ivory in India during the Mughul period :—

Ivory, especially the best kinds, came chiefly from Africa in the first instance.[1] It was, however, also imported from England, though sometimes the commodity was rather dearer in England than in India.[2] The ivory brought from England was not so white as that which came from Mozambique.[3] 'The largest teeth', says Milburn, 'are said to come from Africa, and are most esteemed, being of a closer texture, and less liable to turn yellow than those from the East Indies.'[4]

---

[1] *E.F.I.* 1624-1629, p. XXXV and Milburn, *Oriental Commerce*, I, 62.

[2] *E. F.I.* 1630-1633, p. 5.

[3] *Letters*, III, 10.

[4] Milburn, *Oriental Commerce*, I, 62.

'The ivory from the islands of Ceylon and Achīn [he means Sumatra]', says Tavernier, 'has the peculiarity when it is worked that it never becomes yellow like that from the Peninsula and the West (*sic*) Indies; this causes it to be more esteemed and dearer than the other' (1,222-23). No elephants are found in the West Indies!

So also Ovington: 'The *Achen* Elephants are most looked upon for their Teeth, because that Ivory they say, maintains its Whiteness, and turns not Yellow, as other does' (P. 192).

The elephants of Ceylon, says Linschoten, are the best (I, 80).

These remarks are corroborated by Watt, *Dictionary of the Economic Products of* India:

'It is said that Indian ivory has an opaque dead-white colour, and manifests a tendency to become discoloured. The Ceylon ivory is distinguished by fine grain, small size, and pearly bluish tint. Siam ivory is in the trade regarded as much superior to the Indian in appearance and density. It has been remarked of Africa that the nearer the equator the smaller the elephants but the larger the tusks. The finest *transparent* ivory is collected along the West Coast, between latitudes 10°N. and 10°S. The best *white* ivory is obtained from the East Coast. African ivory is said to be best when recently cut. It has a mellow warm transparent tint, as if soaked in oil, and has very little appearance of grain or texture' (Watt, *Dict.*, III, 227).

We gather from scattered remarks by the John Company factors that the quality of ivory depended on weight, length, and whiteness, as well as on the perfect roundness and soundness of the tusks.[1]

According to Fryer there were three qualities of ivory :

' *Muyn*, such are the greatest, free from Flaws.

Muyda, which are the lesser, or the great ones with Flaws.

---

[1] *Letters*, II, 181 ; III, 10 ; IV, 296.

Sera, the least, or worst sort ' (II, 140).

I am not able to trace the words, *Muyn*, *Muyda* and *Sera* : nor am I able to suggest whether they are of Portuguese or Oriental origin.

' The Weights by which they are bought,' continues Fryer, ' are *Baharrs* and *Frasslees* ; each *Baharr* 20 *Frasslees*, each *Frasslee* 12 *l.* and they call the *Baharrs Gross*.

Of *Muyn*, ½ *Baharr* of 20 *Frasslees*, makes 1 *Baharr Gross*.

Of *Muyda* and *Muyn* they hold equal Price, in regard that though the Teeth of *Muyn* be bigger than the other, yet the *Muyda* giving more Weight, they balance Account' (II, 140).

This means apparently that *Muyn* and *Muyda*—the first and second qualities—were quoted nominally at the same price, but as the *Baharr Gross* of the former was half the weight of the *Baharr Gross* of the latter, the price of the former was really double that of the latter.

Formerly, says Fryer, *Muyn* and *Muyda* were worth 260, 270 and 280 *Cruzado* per *Baharr Gross*. A *Cruzado*, according to Fryer, is $\frac{4}{5}$ of the Roy of $\frac{8}{8}$, or $\frac{8}{5}$ (or $1\frac{3}{5}$) rupees,[1] since a royal (or rial or real) of eight = Rs. 2. The price of a *Baharr Gross* would thus be Rs. 416, 432 and 448 respectively; that is to say, for *Muyn* Rs. 416 to 448 per 120 ℔., and for *Muyda* Rs. 416 to 448 per 240 ℔.

Of the third quality, *Sera*, the current price, says Fryer, is 150, 160 and rarely 180 *Cruzado* per *Baharr Gross*. Presuming that the *Baharr Gross* of this quality was 240 ℔., the quoted price would come to Rs. 240, 256 and 288 respectively for 240 ℔.

Further, at Surat the following rule was observed in the ivory trade: 'All over 16 *Sear* sell at 40 *Sear* to the *Maund*; from 10 to 16, at 60 *Sear* to the *Maund*; from 10 *Sear* and under, 80 *Sear* allowed to the *Maund*' (*Ibid.*).

---

[1] This result is not consistent with the value assigned by Dr. Ball to a crusado, which ranges between 2*s*. 3*d*. and 2*s*. 10*d*. But when we are taking Fryer's statements and weights we must accept his values.

Here the figures refer apparently to the total weight of the particular tusk, a larger one being far more valuable than a smaller one, other things being equal.

As Fryer is talking of Surat, by seer he means presumably the Surat seer, which was $\frac{3}{4}$ of a pound or a little under ; so that 16 seers would be 11 or 12 ℔., and 10 seers about 7℔.

William Milburn, who was in India in the end of the eighteenth and beginning of the nineteenth century, supports this statement, with the further subdivision, that while the tusks weighing from 10 to 5 seers each went 80 seers (or 2 maunds) to the maund, those weighing under 5 seers went 160 seers (*i.e.*, 4 maunds) to the maund (Milburn, *Oriental Commerce*, I, 62).

Milburn also is talking of Surat and Cutch, but he makes his 16 seers equal to 15 ℔., which is an unusual value.

The E. I. Company factors give a widely different scale of weights for the various kinds

Surat factors, writing under date 26 Feb., 1616 [1617], place in the first class tusks weighing two, three, or four to a hundred-weight, in the second those weighing four to eight to a hundredweight, and in the third such as weighed 27 per cwt. (*Letters*, V, 105).

This would assign tusks weighing 28 to 56 ℔. to the first class, those weighing 14 to 28℔. to the second, and those weighing 4 ℔. and under to the third.

Again, we are told that tusks weighing under 16℔. lose a third in value (*E. F. I.* 1651-1654, 140), the hollow of the teeth being worth little (*Letters*, II, 181).

We learn that the medium kinds of ivory found the best market in Gujarāt, while the largest specimens, as one would imagine, were in demand at Agra and Lahore (*Letters*, V, 105). In another place we are told that tusks weighing 16 to 30℔ a piece were most vendible at Surat (*E. F. I.* 1651-1654, p. 140).

The following run of prices can be gathered from the notices in *E. F. I.* and *Letters* :—

Quality	Price in rupees per *Akbari* maund (of 55 ℔.)
Large	40 to 50, with a possible rise to 60.[1]
Medium	30 to 35.[2]
Small	16 to 30.[3]

The smaller sort is called "Chan-dahare."[4]

Linschoten speaks in glowing terms of the skill and workmanship of Cingalese artificers in gold, silver, ivory, iron, and other metals. 'They make the fairest barrels for péeces that may be found in any place,

[1] *E.F.I.* 1622-1623, p. 108;
,, 1624-1629, p. 326;
,, 1630-1633, p. 132;
,, 1646-1650, pp. 8 and 250.
Letters, I, 28, 33 and 238;
II, 100, 218, 248, 260;
III, 8, 86;
IV, 296; V, 105; VI, 159.

[2] *Letters*, III, 41; VI, 159;
E.F.I. 1622-1623, p. 8.

[3] *E.F.I.* 1661-1664, p. 211; *E.F.I.* 1665-1667, p. 31;
Letters, I, 299 and 304;
Letters, V, 105; VI, 159.

[4] *E.F.I.* 1618-1621, p. 189.

which shine as bright as if they were Silver'. The same writer thus describes a crucifix of ivory: 'My maister the Archbishop had a crucifixe of Ivorie of an elle long, presented unto him, by one of the inhabitants of the Ile, and made by him so cunningly and workmanly wrought, that in the hayre, beard, and face, it séemed to be alive, and in al [other parts] so neatly wrought and proportioned in limmes, that the like can not be done in [all] Europe: Whereupon my maister caused it to be put into a case, and sent unto the King of Spaine, as a thing to be wondered at, and worthy of so great a Lord, to be kept among his [costliest] Jewels' (1, 81).

'Their teeth which is the Ivory bone, is much used in India, specially in Cambaia, whereof they make many curious peeces of workemanship, the women weare manillas, or arme bracelets thereof, ten or twelve about each arme, whereby it is there much worne, and are in great numbers brought out of Aethiopia, Mosambique and other places' (Linschoten, II, 3).

In this connection the following passage in the E. F. I. chronicle relating to the Surat

Presidency in 1668 is of interest: 'Elephants teeth have fallen in price these five yeares, and hath not that good esteeme as in former tymes; which made us very inquisitive to finde out the reason, and are told that much of the use they were putt to is taken off; as, uppon the death of the husband, the wife, putting herselfe into widowhood, not onely layes by all her jewells and ornaments, but breakes her ivory bracelетts, which are 8 or 10 uppon each wrist; and soe did the whole kindred, mourning certain dayes, and then were again supplyed with new from the deceaseds kindred; which superstition was soe universall that it caused a vast expense of teeth. But they of late are become wiser and make silver in their stead, which att funeralls they lay by for a tyme and then putt them on again; and this is now become soe generall that little or noe ivory is worne' (*E.F.I.* 1668-1669, p. 26).

Jahāṅgīr tells with his usual unction the story of a slave's workmanship in ivory carving: 'One of the royal slaves who was serving in the seal-cutting departments prepared and laid before me a design such as I had never seen or heard of before. As it is exceedingly strange, a detailed description of it is given. In the shell of a filbert four compartments had been carved out of ivory [strictly, elephant bone]. The first compartment was one of wrestlers, in which two men were engaged in wrestling, a third was standing with a spear in his hand, a fourth with a hard stone ['a stone and a cord', *i.e.*,a sling]. Another was sitting with his hands placed on the ground, while in front of him were laid a piece of wood, a bow and a pot. In the second a throne had been made above which a *shamiyāna* (a tent-fly or canopy) was depicted, and a man of wealth (a prince) was seated on the throne with one leg placed over the other and a pillow at his back. Five servants were standing around and before him, and tree-boughs threw a shade over the throne. In the third compartment is a company of ropedancers, who have raised upright a pole with three ropes fastened to it. A rope-dancer upon it (qu. on the ropes ?) has taken hold of his own right foot with his left hand behind his head, and standing on one foot has placed a goat on the top of the pole.[1] Another person has thrown a drum on his neck and is beating it, whilst another man is standing with his hands lifted up and looking at the rope-dancer. Five other men are also standing, of whom one has a stick in his hand. In the fourth compartment there is a tree, below which the figure of the revered (*ḥaẓrat*) Jesus is shown. One person has placed his head at Jesus' feet, and an old man is conversing with Jesus and four others are standing by. As he had made such a masterpiece, I honoured him with a present and with increased salary' (*Tūzuk*, 97-98; R. &B., I, 200-1).

From the likeness of Jesus Christ in the fourth compartment, Sir Sayyid Aḥmad argues that this piece of carving was probably

[1] The translator makes a correction in the text, which is not warranted by the readings of the MSS. extant. The I.O. MS., to which the translator refers in a footnote, and the finely-written, though incomplete, copy of the *Tūzuk* in the P. U. L., agree with *Iqbālnāma* (p. 58), which reads *buzbāzī*, and not *barbāzī*, as the translator construes it. Sir Sayyid Aḥmad's reading is incorrect. The meaning clearly is that a *buzbāz* is standing and is making a goat stand on the pole, while a person who has a drum round his neck beats it. A *buzbāz* is a performer (quite common in India) who goes about with a goat showing its tricks.

the work of a European artist; the royal slave having got hold of it and passed it off as his own handiwork.

Among the annals of XII R. Y. we read in the *Tūzuk*: 'On this day [Sunday, the 24th *Dai*] Amānat Khān presented two elephants' tusks; they were very large, one of them being 3 cubits 8 *tassū* (finger-breadths) in length and 16 *tassū* in circumference; it weighed 3 maunds and 2 seers, or 24½ Irāq maunds.'[1] At 55 ℔. to the maund, this comes to over 165℔. The weight and size given here may be taken as the maximum weight and size of a tusk in Mughul India. Elsewhere we learn that a tusk weighs up to 200 ℔. That may apply to an African elephant.

Another couple of giant tusks is mentioned below.

The King of Ethopia, Bernier informs us, sent some presents to Aurangzeb at his accession, in token of his goodwill. These included 'a couple of elephants' teeth, of a size so pro-

[1] *Tūzuk*, 209; R. & B., I, 423.
[2] P. 426 above.

digious that it required, it seems, the utmost exertion of a strong man to lift either of them from the ground' (P. 135). None of the presents, however, ever reached Delhi, owing to a series of mishaps on the way.

WALRUS IVORY OR THE "FISH-TEETH"

These are the two long canine teeth or tusks in the upper jaw of the walrus, also called sea-horse or morse. The tusks of the female are slightly longer, though not stouter, than those of the male, and may attain a maximum length of three feet.[1]

The ivory obtained from walrus-tooth is white like elephant ivory, though somewhat more yellowish ; but there seem to have been extant some parti-coloured (veined or spotted) specimens of it, which, when produced before Jahāṅgīr, drew his enthusiastic admiration.

Presents of Khān Daurān from Kābul, which included nine veined (*jauhar-dār*) fish-teeth, have already been given under Chinaware in Mughul India.[2]

---

[1] J. A. Thomson, *New Natural History*, II, 542.
[2] See p. 417 above.

Shāh 'Abbās, King of Persia, had bestowed on "Khān-i-'Ālam" a dagger the hilt of which was made of a walrus-tooth with black spots (or veins). "Khān-i-'Ālam", thinking that the best use he could make of the fine arm was to present it to the Emperor, sent it to court through a servant. The dagger was placed before Jahāñgīr on Thursday, the 20th *Tir*, XIV R. Y. He was delighted with it, and records that it is a rare present, and that he has never seen a spotted specimen of walrus-tooth before. In fact it so whetted his zest for the article that he, ever keen-set for the unusual in nature, sent out men in search of the specimen. But let us hear the rest of the story in his own words: 'A strange circumstance was that I was so much delighted with a jewelled dagger-hilt of piebald teeth which Khān 'Ālam had got from Shāh 'Abbās and sent to me, that I appointed several skilful men to go to Irān and Tūrān to look for them and to be consistently searching for them, and to bring some from anywhere and any person, anyhow, and at any price. Many of my servants who knew my disposition, and dignified Amīrs in the course of their duty, engaged in the search. It happened that in this city a stupid stranger bought in the open bazaar a coloured tooth of great beauty and delicacy for a trifle; he believed that some time or other it had fallen into the fire, and that the black on it was the mark of burning! After some time he showed it to one of the carpenters on the establishment of my prosperous son Shāh-Jahān, desiring that he should take off a piece of the tooth in order to make a ring (*shast*) [rather, thumb-stall worn by archers], and pointed out that he should remove the marks of burning and the blacknesses, being ignorant that the blackness enhanced the value and price of the whiteness. Those moles and patches were what the tire-woman of destiny had given as an adornment of its beauty. The carpenter at once went to the Superintendent of his workshop, and gave him the good news that such a rare and precious thing, in search of which people were wandering and going long distances, and hastening to all corners and in all directions in various countries, had fallen for nothing into the hands of an ignorant man, who did not know its value. It could be easily and cheaply obtained from him. The Superintendent went off with him and immediately procured it, and next day produced it before my son. When my son Shāh Jahān came to wait on me, he at first showed great delight, and after his brain had become free from the intoxication of the wine of joy, produced it, and greatly pleased me'—

May thy time be happy that thou hast made mine happy!

'I invoked so many blessings on him that if one of them out of a hundred obtain acceptance, it will suffice for his spiritual and material well-being' (*Tūzuk*, 275; R. & B., II, 96).

The story is continued a page or so lower: 'On the 1st of the Divine month, out of the veined (*jauhar-dār*) spotted tooth (walrus) which my son Shāh-Jahān had given me as an offering, I ordered to be cut off sufficient for two dagger-hilts and a thumb-stall: it came out of a beautiful colour and was very choice. I ordered the *Ustāds* (masters) Pūran and Kalyān, who had no rivals in the art of engraving, to make dagger-hilts of a shape that was approved at this time, and has become known as the Jahāṅgīrī fashion. At the same time the blade and the sheath and fastenings were given to skilful men, each of whom was unique in his age in his art. Truly, it was all carried out according to my wish. One hilt came out coloured in such a way as to create astonishment. It turned out of all the seven colours, and some of the flowers looked as if a skilful painter had depicted them in black lines round it with a wonder-working pencil. In short, it was so-delicate that I never wish it to be apart from me for a moment. Of all the gems of great price that are in the treasury I consider it the most precious. On Thursday I girded it auspiciously and with joy round my waist, and the masters who in their completion had exercised great skill and taken great pains were rewarded. Ustād Pūran with the gift of an elephant, a dress of honour, and a golden bracelet for the wrist, which the people of India caḷl *Kara*, and Kalyān with the title of ' Ajā'ib-dast (wondrous hand), and increased mansab, a dress of honour, and a jewelled bracelet (*pahūnchī*), and in the same way every one according to his circumstances and skill received favours' (*Tūzuk*, 276-77; R. & B., II, 98-99).

But this was not the end of the matter. The vigorous search for the " fish-teeth " which the Emperor instituted soon bore fruit in another quarter. In the annals of the next year he has the following information to give us: 'As at this time I was much inclined to parti-coloured veined teeth, the great Amirs exerted themselves greatly in looking out for them. Of these, 'Abdu-l-'Azīz K. Naqshbandī sent a servant of the name of 'Abdu-llah with a letter to Khwāja Ḥasan and Khwāja 'Abdu-r-Raḥīm, ss. Khwāja Kalān Jūybārī, who are to-day the leading holy men of Transoxiana, containing a request for these things. By chance Khwāja Hasan had a perfect tooth, exceedingly delicate, and immediately sent it with the aforesaid (servant) to the Court, which it reached this day. I was greatly pleased, and ordered them to send the value of Rs. 30,000 in choice goods to the Khwājas, a service for which Mīr Baraka Bukhārī was fixed upon' (*Tūzuk*, 310; R. & B., II, 166).

The translator thinks that tortoise-shell, and not walrus-tooth, is referred to in these passages; because 'there is nothing black or piebald about walrus-teeth, and Jahāṅgīr would surely not admire greatly a kind of ivory which was inferior to that of the elephant' (II, 94, f. n.). I am rather inclined to think that what is meant *is* walrus-teeth. We cannot imagine that Indian emperors did not know the difference between walrus-tooth and tortoise-shell. And it was just because walrus-tooth is usually white, and just because the particular specimens obtained bore the beautiful black-and-white veins or spots (which, he says, are rare), that Jahāṅgīr was so enthusiastic over them, and was so keen for more.[1]

On Thursday, the 15th *Ābān*, XIV R. Y., Jahāṅgīr presented to Sulṭān Parwīz a *tupchāq* horse, a waist-dagger with a black-and-white *jauhardār* handle [of walrus-tooth], a *khāṣṣa* sword and a *khāṣṣa* shield (*Tūzuk*, 280).

TORTOISE-SHELL

It consists of the horny plates of the hawks-bill turtle (*Chelonia imbricata*), the smallest

[1] See Addendum on p. 300 of R. & B., II.

of the sea turtles. These plates 'are harder, more brittle and less fibrous than ordinary horn. Their value depends on the rich mottled colours they display—a warm translucent yellow, dashed and spotted with rich brown tints—and on the high polish they take and retain. The finest tortoiseshell is obtained from the Eastern Archipelago, particularly from the east coast of Celebes to New Guinea; large supplies come from the West Indian islands and Brazil' (*Enc. Brit.*, XXII, p. 310).

'Tortoiseshell,' continues the writer of the same article, 'has been a prized ornamental material from very early times. It was one of the highly esteemed treasures of the Far East brought to ancient Rome by way of Egypt, and it was eagerly sought by wealthy Romans as a veneer for their rich furniture. In modern times it is most characteristically used in the elaborate inlaying of cabinetwork known as buhl furniture, and in combination with silver for toilet articles. It is also employed as a veneer for small boxes and frames. It is cut into combs, moulded into snuff-boxes and other small boxes, formed into knife-handles, and worked up into many other similar minor articles. The plates from certain other tortoises, known commercially as turtle-shell, possess a certain industrial value, but they are either opaque or soft and leathery, and cannot be mistaken for tortoise-shell. A close imitation of tortoise-shell can be made by stain ing translucent horn or by varieties of celluloid' (*Ibid.*).

'Torteauxes [tortoises] there are likewise in great numbers throughout all India: of their shelles they make many curious devises, as Combes, Cuppes, and Boles to drinke in, with tablemen [men at backgammon] and divers such like thinges, knowing howe to give it a faire and shining colour most pleasant to behold, and is more esteemed of in India, then the mother of pearle, by reason of the beautiful colour they set uppon it' (Linschoten, II, 136). The same writer in another place speaks of shields made of tortoise-shell 'wrought and inlaide very workemanlike' (*Ibid.*, I, 61).

Tortoise-shell seems to have come mainly from Bantam, and also from Ceylon.[1]

The Sūrat factors declare that the blackest colour and thickest shells are most in request.[2]

Sūrat quotations extending from 1619 to 1649 give a nearly uniform price of just over two rupees a seer (of 7/10℔.).[3]

When the shell of a single animal weighed 1½ or 2℔., says Fryer, it sold for 30 or 36 *cruzado* per *frasslee* (II, 140). This price comes to Rs. 48 to 57⅜ per *frasslee*.

We assume the *frasslee* to be equal to about 22½℔., which is the usual value; although on the same page, in connection with ivory, Fryer makes the *frasslee*=12℔., which is presumably the special value of the *frasslee* of ivory.

---

[1] *E.F.I* 1634-1636, pp. 49 and 296;
„ 1642-1645, pp. 86 and 211;
„ 1655-1660, p. 56.

[2] *E.F.I.* 1618-1621, p. 55.

[3] *E.F.I.* 1618-1621, p. 55;
„ 1642-1645, p. 211;
„ 1646-1650, p. 234.

This calculation would yield the price $2\frac{1}{2}$ rupees to the pound —a rate which tallies roughly with that deduced from the factors' reports (given above); although Fryer's time is late in the century, *viz.*, 1672-81.

MISCELLANEOUS

As a supplement to the above are appended the following notices of articles made of ivory, tortoise-shell, ebony, jet, amber, and crystal:

Linschoten, speaking of the industries and trade of Cambay, says that there are found there 'fine playing tables, and Chessebordes of Ivory, and shields of Torteur shelles, wrought and inlaide very workemanlike, many fayre signets, ringes, and other curious worke of Ivorie, and sea horse téeth, as also of Amber, whereof there is great quantitie: They have likewise a kind of mountain Christall, wherof they make many signets, buttons, beades, and divers other devises' (I, 61).

Roe thus narrates the presents he made to Āghā Nūr, the *Kotwāl* of Agra, who, he says, was one of his best friends:

'I gave him according to the custome two knives, one of amber and one of jett, cost x*s*., and a pare of tables of ebonie and eliphants tooth, worth 30*s*. Then hee desired mee to give his brother a pare of knives, which I did, of vi*s*. price. After that hee desired some greater knives, and I shewed him fower, which hee tooke every one, without restooring the former. Though this was somewhat unmannerly, yet I was content, because hee is one of the best frends wee have in India and did keepe the English house from being taken from them in Agra' (Roe, 143, f. n. 1).

Tavernier's general remarks about the course of trade in coral and lapis lazuli beads, yellow amber, tortoise-shell, etc., are interesting.

'Those merchants who come from Bhutān and Kābul go to Kandahār and on to Ispahān, and they generally take back coral beads, yellow amber, and lapis wrought into beads when they can obtain them. The other merchants, returning from the regions about Multān, Lahore, and Agra, take calicoes, indigo, and an abundance of carnelian and crystal beads. Finally, those who return by

Gorakhpur, and have an understanding with the customs officer, take from Patna and Dacca coral, yellow amber, tortoise-shell bracelets, and others of sea shells, with numerous round and square pieces of the size of our 15-sol coins, which are also of the same tortoise-shell and sea shells. When I was at Patna four Armenians, who had previously made a journey to the Kingdom of Bhutān, came from Dantzic, where they had had made numerous images of yellow amber, which represented all kinds of animals and monsters; these they were taking to the King of Bhutān to place in his pagodas, he being, like his people, exceedingly idolatrous. Wherever the Armenians see that money is to be made they have no scruple about supplying materials for the purposes of idolatry, and they told me that if they had been able to get an idol made which the King had ordered from them they would have been enriched. It was a head in the form of a monster, which had six horns, four ears, and four arms, with six fingers on each hand, the whole to be of yellow amber, but the Armenians could not find sufficiently large pieces for the purpose' (Tavernier, II, 203-204).

SOME CURIOSITIES

We have so far dealt with substances and articles commonly known and recognized as useful or ornamental. But there is another class of things which stands by itself. Some substances were credited in good old days with certain curative and other properties, for which they were highly prized. They are interesting as a study in superstitions that we have outlived. Indeed, there is something picturesque about the ignorant credulity of a great and civilized people, to whom we owe so much. And yet who knows, there may be some stray particles of truth in popular superstitions and exploded beliefs.

(1) Rhinoceros-horn

Mysterious properties were supposed to belong to the horn of the rhinoceros from ancient times.

The medical dictionaries like the *Muḥīt-i-Aʿẓam* tell us in detail how various diseases could be cured, some by the patient wearing a ring cut out of the horn, others by grinding the horn and drinking the juice, or again by drinking from a cup made of it, or else through vapours rising from the horn held on fire (*Muḥīṭ-i-A'ẓam*, Cawnpore, 1313 *A.H.*, IV, p. 61).

Cups made of rhinoceros-horn indicated the presence of poison, and were consequently held in high esteem among nations where poisoning was a common form of taking life. Besides drinking-cups, knife-handles and rings were carved out of the horn.

'*Ajā'ibu'l-Makhlūqāt* has a long article on the rhinoceros, where the wonderful properties of its horn are set out in detail.

We find there was a similar belief current in the West, which continued down to the seventeenth century; but there the horn was known as the "unicorn's horn"; that is to say, the Europeans ascribed imaginary properties to the horn of an imaginary animal. This was natural enough, since we know that the rhinoceros did not exist in Europe.

We learn from Fuller's *Worthies of England* that there was a "unicorn's horn" in the

Tower as well as another in Windsor Castle. As for its properties, he says, it is reputed to be not only an antidote against several poisons, but it resists 'poisons which kill by second qualities, that is, by corrosion of parts.' Dr. Fuller himself heard a report of a successful experiment made with it, where some grains of the horn proved an effective antidote against poison.[1]

Whether these horns were of the rhinoceros, or of the narwhal, or of some other animal, is entirely a matter of conjecture.

It has been remarked that the belief about the properties of a "unicorn's horn" was later transferred to the horn of the rhinoceros, when no unicorn was found to exist.[2] Obviously this cannot apply to the eastern peoples, who from the beginning stuck to the rhinoceros, and in whose mythology the unicorn had no place.

---

[1] Thomas Fuller, *History of the Worthies of England*, London, 1840, II, 338 and 340.

[2] Linschoten, II, p. 9, footnote 2.

But we are concerned chiefly with the rhinoceros-horn in Mughul India and the popular belief about its virtues in that country.

After describing the rhinoceros and its horn, Linschoten says: 'The Portingales and those of Bengala affirme, that by the River Ganges in the Kingdome of Bengala, are many of these Rhinoceros, which when they will drinke, the other beasts stand and waite upon them, till the Rhinoceros hath drunke, and thrust their horne into the water, for he cannot drink but his horne must be under the water because it standeth so close unto his nose, and muzzle: and then after him all the other beastes doe drinke. Their hornes in India are much esteemed and used against all venime, poyson, and many other diseases: likewise his teeth, clawes, flesh, skin and blood, and his very dung, and water and all whatsoever is about him, is much esteemed in India, and used for the curing of many diseases and sicknesses, which is very good and most true, as I my selfe by experience have found; but it is to be understood, that all Rhinocerotes are not a like good, for there are some whose hornes are sold for one, two, or three hundred pardawes the peece, and there are others of the same colour and greatnes that are sold but for three or foure Pardawes, which the Indians know and can discerne. The cause is that some Rhinocerotes, which are found in certaine places in the countrie of Bengala have this vertue, by reason of the hearbes which that place only yeeldeth and bringeth foorth, which in other places is not so, and this estimation is not onely held of the horne, but of all other things in his whole body, as I saide before (II, 9-10).

William Finch has the following: 'Here [near Ajodhyā] is great Trade, and such abundance of Indian Asse-horne, that they make hereof Bucklers, and divers sorts of Drinking Cups. There are of these Hornes, all the Indians affirme, some rare of great price, no Jewell comparable, some esteeming them the right Unicornes Horne' (Purchas, IV, 66).

'Great Prices', says Fryer, 'are offered for those [rhinoceros-horns] that are inadulterate; which they in *India* pretend to try by the

Liquors presently fermenting in them; but notwithstanding that Experiment they are often deceived by false Horns made into drinking Cups' (II, 298).

'They ascribe very much likewise to the Rhinoceros Horn in *India*', says Ovington, 'as it is an Antidote against all poysonous Draughts, and hugely extol in it that Medicinal Excellence and singular Quality. The Character of this Horn prevail'd so far with a former President of ours at *Suratt*, that he exchang'd for a Cup made of this Horn a large capacious Silver Bowl of the same bigness.'[1]

We read in an Armenian's report that 'there are many beasts with one horn in their forehead like unto an unicorn, which horn they say is good against poison, there are of them which weigh 8 ℔., some 7, 6, 4, and 3 ℔., the greatest and fairest worth some 4 rials per piece, and those of a lesser sort worth less. Amongst the Turks and Moors in Arabia every ℔. is worth one rial of 8' (*Letters*, I, 193).

---

[1] Ovington, *Voyage to Suratt*, London, 1696, p. 297.

Bābur tells us that 'out of one of the largest of these horns I had a drinking-vessel made, and a dice-box, and about three or four fingers' bulk of it might be left' (*Memoirs of Bābur.* tr. Leyden, Erskine and King, II, 210).

Sir Thomas Roe once laid a nice little plot against Prince S͟hāh Jahān. He tried to win his good graces by offering him a "unicorn's horne" at a price, pretending that he did not speak of it to Jahāṅgīr since he wanted to give him (the Prince) an opportunity of securing it and offering it in due course to the Emperor. The ambassador spoke in glowing terms of the virtues of the horn, and represented that it was so valuable that he had no power to sell it, and that the merchants made a secret of it, and did not allow it to come out of the ship. He made an offer, however, that if the Prince wished to buy it and would accede to certain demands of Sir Thomas's then pending, he could let the Prince's officer see the horn. 'This I hoped,' continues the ambassador, ever a clever diplomat, and at this moment at his best, 'would both sett an extreame appetite on the Prince to passe it at a high price, and would insinuate an extraordinary desire in mee to doe him service ; and if hee reavealed it to the King, I would answere : because it was not in my power to give His Majestie, I was ashamed to name yt, but had mooved the Prince to buy it for his use' (P. 255).

The Prince, always a match for the tactician, was in this case too clever for him. He returned formal thanks, but matters proceeded no further.

The above entry is under October 16,1616. Eight months later Roe records that 'the unicornes horne was returned as without vertue' (P. 366). It was then sent on to Sūrat and then to Ahmadābād, where John Browne, a factor, showed it to Muqarrab Khān, asking 5,000 rupees for it. The factor says that he tried the efficacy of the horn on the lives of 'a pigeon, goate, and man, which they loosing, itt also lost his esteeme, and soe I returned it aboard from whence I had ytt.'[1]

---

[1] *E. F. I.* 1618-1621, p. 12.

Muqarrab Khān not buying it, the horn was sent to Achin,[1] and then on to Bantam.[2] Finally it passed into the hands of the Dutch, and was sold in Holland for £400.[3]

(2) Bezoar-stone

Bezoar-stone (from Pers. *pād-zahr*, lit., protecting from poison, *i.e.*, an antidote) is a concretion found in the stomach and intestines of ruminants and some other animals. We are here concerned only with the Oriental species, and not with the Occidental, which is obtained from the llamas of Peru, nor with the German, which is obtained from the chamois.

We may note in passing, however, that Ben Jonson had heard of the bezoar-stone: 'Body o'me, a shrewd mischance! why, had you no unicorn's horn, nor bezoar's stone about you, ha?' (*Every Man out of his Humour*, V, 4).

[1] *E. F. I.* 1618-1621, p. 58.
[2] *Ibid.*, p. 184.
[3] *Ibid.*, p. 11, f. n.

The Oriental bezoar was supposed to possess powerful medicinal qualities, being specially used as an antidote in Persia, India and other eastern countries.

Dr. Kunz tells us that a bezoar-stone upon which a scorpion's figure had been engraved during the time when the constellation Scorpio was in the ascendant, was considered an effective cure for a scorpion's bite (*Curious Lore of Precious Stones*, 340).

This intestinal calculus appears to have been in great request in India, and the early European travellers (including Garcia da Orta) seem to believe in its efficacy not only as an antidote, but as a useful therapeutic agent and an aphrodisiac.

The Oriental bezoar is found in the wild goat of Persia and in various kinds of antelopes. But we are specially concerned with India, about which information from contemporary observers is available :

In this country, in the seventeenth and eighteenth centuries, the bezoar was obtainable chiefly from goats, but also from cows and monkeys, and geographically was strictly localized.

The following is from Linschoten :—'The Bezar stone commeth out of Persia, from the land or Province called Carassone [Khurāsān], and also out of other places in India : they grow within the maw of a sheepe or Goat, about a little straw, that lyeth in the middle [of the maw], for by experience the straw is often found within them : the stone is very slicke & smooth without, of a darke greene colour' (II, 142).

'This Bezars stone is very costly, and is much used in India against all poyson, and [other] diseases, and is more esteemed then Unicornes horne, in Europe, for it is much tryed and sold very deare : the greater and heavier they are, the better and of more vertue they are : the common sorte are of three foure or five octaves weight, some more, some lesse : they are much brought into Portingal, and greatly esteemed : the place where they are most found, is (as I said before) in Persia and also in the Island called Insula das Vacas, or the Island of Cowes: It lyeth before the mouth of the river, entering into Cambaia, hard by the coast where the Portingall navie often putteth in to refresh themselves, and [being there], kill divers of the sheepe or Goats, wherein they finde many of these Bezars stones: likewise in the lande of Pan [Pahang] by Malacca there are many found' (*Ibid.*, 143-44).

'The Bezars stone is as hard as [any] stone, but not very heavie: It is thought that these stones doe grow in the mawes of sheepe by vertue of the grasse [or hearbes] whereon they pasture and feed, as we have declared of the Rhinoceros, because they doe onely breede in those places above named, and in no place els, where these kinds of beastes are' (144).

One of the quotations in *Hobson-Jobson* (91*a*) runs as follows:—'The King of Bantam sends K. James I. "two *beasar* stones"'.—Sainsbury, I, 143.

Manucci tells us how he once fed on chicken-broth and bezoar-stone a patient who had been weakened with enema and purgatives. The patient, who was a *qāẓī's* wife, steadily gained strength, and was, in a few days, restored to perfect health (*Storia*, II, 178).

Roe, Tavernier, and Manucci seem to agree that the bezoar-stone was found in what is now the Masulipatam district in the Madras presidency; though Manucci is quite wrong in deriving the name *pād-zahr* from Bezwada in that district. Manucci says that in that part the goats are 'very numerous', and that 'the goat-herds who tend them are aware of how many [bezoar-stones] there are in each goat, and the weight of each' (*Storia*, II, 431).

Roe adds Bengal as another Indian locality. But his remarks are worth quoting in full. 'For Bezars', he says, 'ther are threе sorts ; the best are of Persia, others from Malacca, the last of Masolapatan and Bengala......The best ......are a blackish greene of Persia..........The prices in England are about 3 *li.* an ounce ; if the stones be great and whole they are woorth 5 *li.*.....To avoid counterfaytes...........with a very hot needles poynt peck them. If it make noe signe, they are not false ; if the nedle enter or burne them, they are made ones. The best triall of the virtue is to lay them in buffles, milke, and the best will turne it like runnett and those are rich' (Roe, 157, f.n. 1).

We are told in the *Relations of Golconda* that where they are found, the bezoar-goats are killed for their skins and the stones in large numbers, so that the flesh is mostly thrown away. Two, three, and sometimes as many as four small stones are found in a single goat, some long, others round in shape. The concretion forms round a woody nucleus (P. 34).

From an experiment reported in the same place one may infer that the formation of a bezoar-stone depends more upon the kind of vegetation on which the goat feeds in that region, than on any peculiarity of the species (P. 35). This seems to be corroborated by Tavernier who refers to a particular tree on which the goats feed, though, he says, he has forgotten the name of it. 'This plant,' he continues, 'bears little buds, about which, and also on the tips of the branches, which the goats eat, the bezoar concretes in the bellies of these animals. It assumes a form according to the shape of the buds and the ends of the branches, and this is why one finds it in so many different shapes. The peasants, by feeling the belly of the goat, know how many bezoars it contains, and they sell the goat for a price in proportion to the number which are therein. In order to ascertain this, they run both hands under the belly of the goat and beat the paunch along both sides, so that all the stones fall to the middle, and they then estimate exactly, by touch, how many bezoars are in it. The value of bezoar depends on the size, although the small possess no less virtue than the large. But in this respect one is often deceived by the fact that there are people who enlarge the bezoar with a kind of paste made of gum and other materials of the same colour as the bezoar. They understand, even, how to give as many coats as the natural bezoar ought to have. One can detect this fraud easily by two methods. The first by weighing the bezoar and placing it to steep for some time in lukewarm water; if the water does not change its colour, and if the bezoar does not lose weight, it has not been adulterated. The other means is to touch the bezoar with a pointed hot iron; if the iron enters it and makes it fry, it is a sign that it is a mixture, and that it is not genuine. For the rest, the larger the bezoar the higher the price, which rises in proportion like that of the diamond. For if 5 or 6 bezoars weigh an ounce, the ounce will be worth from 15 to 18 francs, but if it is a bezoar of one ounce, the ounce will be worth fully 100 francs. I have sold one of 4¼ ounces for as much as 2,000 livres [£150]' (Tavernier, II, 116).

These prices work out as follows:

Weight of single stone.	Price.
$\frac{1}{6}$ to $\frac{1}{5}$ of an oz.	2*s*. to 2*s*. 10½ *d*.
1 oz.	£4.
4¼ oz.	£150.

We have seen that Roe quotes £3 to £5 an oz. as the price in England, which is considerably lower. This is vague, but it may support Fryer's statement that owing to a heavy demand in India the stones cannot be bought there to yield profit in England enough to repay for the trouble (Fryer, II, 34).

William Methwold bought at Masulipatam in 1621 a few bezoar-stones, some at 24 rialls (=48 rupees) per seer (of 12 oz.) and some dearer (*E. F. I.* 1618-1621, p. 255).

In a communication dated Jan. 6, 1648, from Sūrat, we have the following remark :—'Bezoar stones cannot be got from Golconda (where the "pagode" is now worth, exchange included, 4¾ rupees) under 33 and 36 mahmūdīs per ounce' (*E. F. I.* 1646-1650, p. 182). So the price at Golconda was Rs. 13 or 14 per oz.—a very high price compared with the last quotation; but we may explain it by supposing that here the stones were larger, and therefore much more costly;—besides the dates are 27 years apart.

Again, in a Sūrat report for 1668, Rs. 3½ per *tola* is quoted for bezoar-stone. This is equivalent to Rs. 8¾ per oz. (*E. F. I.* 1668-1669, p. 3).

Tavernier visited Golconda several times and was interested in the bezoar-goats. He once purchased as much as about 60,000 rupees' worth of bezoar for the servants of the English and Dutch Companies. Considering Roe's quotation and Fryer's remark, the English could not have bought it for importation to England. Possibly they did so for local disposal.

It appears that export of bezoar-goats from Golconda was prohibited on pain of death, the king of Golconda farming out the trade for a yearly payment of 6,000 old pagodas, or 45,000 livres.[1] It was with great difficulty, therefore, that Tavernier once succeeded in procuring six bezoar-goats, which he examined at his leisure. 'They are beautiful animals', he says, 'very tall, and having fine hair, like silk.' He had to pay 3 rupees for a goat with one bezoar only, 4 rupees each for another two, and 4¼ each for the remaining three. The last five had from two to four bezoars each (Tavernier, II, 116-18).

Jahāṅgīr relates that an Afg͟hān once 'brought from the Carnatic two goats that had *pāzahar* (bezoar stones, an antidote against

---

[1] This equation is untenable on Tavernier's own showing; since 6,000 old pagodas=£2,700, and 45,000 livres=£3,375. But with Tavernier this is a small matter.

poison). I had always heard that an animal that has pazahar is very thin and miserable, but these goats were very fat and fresh. I ordered them to kill one of them, which was a female. Four pazahar stones became apparent, and this caused great astonishment' (*Tūzuk*, 117; R. & B., 1, 240). The Carnatic, as the reader is aware, borders on Golconda.

Bezoars are also obtained from cows, which weigh up to 17 or 18 French ounces. But these are not esteemed. A bezoar from a monkey, which is round in shape, is particularly efficacious, but rare, and proportionately costly. One of the size of a nut would cost more than 100 écus (*i.e.*, £22-10-0) (Tavernier, II, 118-19).

Methwold (*Relations of Golconda*, 34) and Fryer (II, 141) are at one with Tavernier in thinking that the monkey bezoars are the best; though Fryer says they are long, while Tavernier makes them round. 'Those that are rough', continues Fryer, 'prove commonly faulty, breaking with Stones in the middle: Others in form of Tares, somewhat flat, which break in smaller Stones in the middle, are better than the rough ones' (*Ibid.*).

Manucci has the following interesting, if fantastic, account of the origin of the bezoar in monkeys: 'They [the monks] told me that in that country [Borneo] was an island where there were many baboons. The natives inflict wounds on them with a small poisoned arrow shot from a *zarvatana* (blow-tube). The baboon, aware that the wound is poisoned, takes to flight at once, and goes to find a certain herb which is an antidote. The blood is then stanched and the wound closes, but at the spot, instead of flesh, the blood congeals into a stone which possesses the virtue of the plant that was eaten. The natives recognise these baboons by their height, and killing them, withdraw the stone which has greater potency than any others' (*Storia*, III, 191-92).

Fryer suggests the following methods of detecting fraudulent manufactures: '*Bezcar* is tried sundry ways: As the rubbing Chalk upon a Paper, then rubbing the Stone hard upon the Chalk, if it leave an Olive-Colour it is good. Also touch any with a Red-hot Iron, which you suspect because their Colour is lighter than ordinarily they use to be, and if they fry like Resin or Wax, they are naught. Sometimes they are tried by putting them into clear Water, and if there arise upon them small white Bubbles, they are good, and if none, they are doubtful. The use of the Hot Iron is esteemed infallible' (II, 141).

The reader will notice that at least one test, *viz.*, that of the pointed hot iron, is common to Roe, Tavernier and Fryer, and the last writer calls it infallible.

(3) PORCUPINE STONE

The bezoar leads on naturally to the 'porcupine stone', which was another much-esteemed antidote, and, according to Tavernier, 'more efficacious against poison than bezoar.' It was found in the head of the porcupine. 'When it is placed to steep in water for a quarter of an hour,' continues Tavernier, 'the water becomes so bitter that there is nothing in the world to equal it in bitterness. This animal has also sometimes, in its belly, a stone which is of the same nature and equally good as that which comes from the head, except with this difference, that it loses nothing of its weight or size by steeping in water, while there is diminution of the other. During my life I have bought three of these stones. One cost me 500 écus [£112-10-0], and I disposed of it subsequently with advantage to the Ambassador Dominico de Santis, of whom I have spoken in my accounts of Persia. I paid 400 écus [£ 90] for another, which I still keep; and the third was sold to me for 300 écus [£67-10-0], and I made a present of it to a friend' (Tavernier, II, 119-20).

The editor's footnote to this passage is worth quoting: 'It seems probable that the substance supposed to be obtained in the head of the porcupine was a vegetable drug, to which that mythical origin was ascribed (Garcia da Orta, 470 f.). Castanheda mentions a stone obtained in the head of an animal called bulgoldorf, which was exceedingly rare, and was said to be an antidote against all kinds of poison (Kerr, *Voyages and Travels*, ii, 439). A. Hamilton (in Pinkerton, viii, 450) says that at Lingen, near Johore, he has seen pieces of porcupine bezoar as big as, and shaped like, a walnut, valued at 600 pieces of eight.' It is only necessary to add that a piece of eight had the same value as an *écu*, *viz.*, 4*s.* 6*d.*

(4) SNAKE-STONE

Hobson-Jobson has the following: 'This is a term applied to a substance, the application of which to the part where a snake-bite has taken effect, is supposed to draw out the poison and render it innocuous. Such applications are made in various parts of the Old and New Worlds. The substances which have this reputation are usually of a porous kind, and when they have been chemically examined have proved to be made of charred bone, or the like. There is an article in the 13th vol. of the *Asiatic Researches* by Dr. J. Davy, entitled *An Analysis of the Snake-Stone*, in which the results of the examination of three different kinds, all obtained from Sir Alex. Johnstone, Chief Justice of Ceylon, is given. (1) The first kind was of round or oval form, black or brown in the middle, white towards the circumference, polished and somewhat lustrous, and pretty enough to be sometimes worn as a neck ornament; easily cut with a knife, but not scratched by the nail. When breathed on it emitted an earthy smell, and when applied to the tongue, or other moist surface, it adhered firmly. This kind proved to be of bone partially calcined. (2) We give below a quotation regarding the second kind. (3) The third was apparently a *bezoar*, rather than a snake-stone' (P. 847*b*). The quotation referred to under No. 2 is from Dr. Davy's *Asiatic Researches*, xiii, 318, and runs as follows: 'Another kind of *snake-stone*......was a small oval body, smooth and shining, externally black, internally grey; it had no earthy smell when breathed on, and had no absorbent or adhesive power. By the person who presented it to Sir Alexander Johnstone it was much valued, and for adequate reason if true, "it had saved the lives of four men"' (P. 848*b*).

There seem to be two kinds of snake-stones: (1) Artificial, and (2) Natural:—

(1) *Artificial snake-stone.*—A kind of artificial snake-stone manufactured in Diu is thus described by Thevenot: 'C'est dans cette Ville de Diu que se font les *Pierres de Cobra* si renommées: elles sont composées de racines qu'on brûle, et dont on

amasse les cendres pour les mettre avec une sorte de terre qu'ils ont, et les brûler encore une fois avec cette terre ; et après cela on en fait la pâte dont ces Pierres sont formées...... Il faut faire sortir avec une éguille, un peu de sang de la plaie, y appliquer la Pierre, et l'y laisser jusqu'à ce qu'elle tombe d'elle même'.—Thevenot, v. 97.[1]

Fryer speaks of 'the Venom of a certain Snake, for which the *Jangies* [*Jogis*] or Pilgrims furnish them [the Christians on the Malabar Coast] with a Factitious Stone (which we call a Snake-stone) and is Counterpoyson to all deadly Bites ; if it stick, it attracts the Poyson ; and put it into Milk, it recovers it self again, leaving its virulency therein, discovered by its Greenness.'[2]

Tavernier winds up his long account of miscellaneous stones with the following passage : 'I shall finally make mention of the snake-stone, which is nearly the size of a double [? doubloon, a Spanish gold coin, larger than the English

[1] This quotation is copied from *Hobson-Jobson*, the French text of de Thevenot being not available to me.

[2] Fryer, I, 138-39.

penny, formerly worth 33 to 36s., now slightly over £1], some of them tending to an oval shape, being thick in the middle and becoming thin towards the edges. The Indians say that it grows on the heads of certain snakes, but I should rather believe that it is the priests of the idolaters who make them think so, and that this stone is a composition which is made of certain drugs. Whatever it may be, it has an excellent virtue in extracting all the poison when one has been bitten by a poisonous reptile. If the part bitten is not punctured it is necessary to make an incision so that the blood may flow; and when the stone has been applied to it, it does not fall off till it has extracted all the venom which is drawn to it. In order to clean it it is steeped in woman's milk, or, in default of it, in that of a cow; and after having been steeped for ten or twelve hours, the milk, which has absorbed all the venom, assumes the colour of matter. One day, when I dined with the Archbishop of Goa, he took me into his museum, where he had many curiosities. Among other things he showed me one of these stones, and in telling me of its properties assured me that but three days since he had made trial of it, and then he presented it to me. As he traversed a marsh on the island of Salsette, upon which Goa is situated, on his way to a house in the country, one of his pallankeen bearers, who was almost naked, was bitten by a serpent and was at once cured by this stone. I have bought many of them; it is only the Brahmans who sell them, and it is that which makes me think that they make them. You employ two methods to ascertain if the snake-stone is good, and that there is no fraud. The first is by placing the stone in the mouth, for then, if good, it leaps and attaches itself immediately to the palate. The other is to place it in a glass full of water, and immediately, if it is genuine, the water begins to boil, and small bubbles ascend from the stone which is at the bottom, to the top of the water' (Tavernier, II, 120-21).

Ovington tells a story of a snake-bite and the cure of it effected with a snake-stone, which he follows up with a description of composition and virtues of a snake-stone, and the methods of putting it to the test: 'A Peon of mine, named *Gemal*,' he says, 'walking abroad in the

Grass after the Rains, was unfortunately bit on a sudden by one of them. The latent Snake twisted unawares about his Leg, and in a short time brought him to the Ground, by causing in him an immediate deliquium of Spirit, almost even to Expiration. The Servants who were standing by, amaz'd at the accident, called immediately upon an *English* Merchant, who hasten'd towards him with a special Medicine for his Recovery. The thing which he carried about him, and which instantly applyed, is a Specifick against the Poison of Snakes, cured him, and therefore obtains the Name of Snake-stone. It is a small artificial Stone, almost flat, only with a little protuberance in the middle, and of a gray Colour. The Composition of it is Ashes of burnt Roots, mixt with a kind of Earth, which is found at *Diu*, belonging to the *Portuguese* ; and those are burnt together again, out of which Paste the Stones are formed. They are not all alike Colour'd, but those that have receiv'd more of the Fire, are thereby inclin'd to a lighter Gray, the others are a little more dark. This Stone Cures by the application of it to the part invenom'd, to which it immediately sticks fast, and by its powerful Attraction sucks back the infus'd Venom, 'till its Pores are full. Then like a glutted Horse-Leach it falls off, and disgorges the replenisht Pores in Milk (the properest liquor for this purpose) which by discolouring, it renders livid. Upon this it recovers new strength, and its Alexipharmick quality again, and is speedily prepar'd for a fresh Draught of Poison, if any remains in the affected part, 'till it quite extracts whatever the venomous Serpent had immited; which makes those Counterpoisons in great esteem against all external Attacks upon the Body; as the Cordial Antidotes are most valuable for expelling or subduing any Poyson inwardly receiv'd. The double Excellence of this Stone recommends its worth very highly, in that a little of it scraped off, and mixt with Wine, or some other proper vehicle, and inwardly taken, is reputed one of the most powerful Medicines against any Malignant Fevers or Infectious Diseases, that is known; and much excels the deservedly fam'd *Gasper Antoni*, or Goa Stone. The trial of these Stones is made by fixing them to the Roof of the Mouth, to which if they stick fast, 'tis a sign they are genuine, if they easily fall off, fictitious. Another method for knowing the true Stones from the Counterfeit, is to immerse them in a Glass of Water, where, after a while, if some light Ebullitions rise from them, and ascend through the Body of the Water, this likewise is an approv'd Sign that the Stone is not spurious. The *Europeans*, for the Security of themselves against the Danger of these Serpents, which are every where so common in *India*, carry always about them one of these Stones inclosed in a Heart of Gold, fixt to a Golden Chain, which hangs about their Necks' (P. 260-63).

The reader will have remarked that the author is speaking here of the artificial snake-stone. He knows nothing apparently of the 'natural' snake-stone.

The following quotation is taken from *Hobson-Jobson*, as it stands: 'The use of the *Pamboo-Kaloo*, or *snake-stone*, as a remedy in cases of wounds by venomous serpents, has probably been communicated to the Singhalese by the itinerant snake-charmers who resort to the island from the Coast of Coromandel; and more than one well-authenticated instance of its successful application has been told to me by persons who had been eye-witnesses'......... (These follow.) '......As to the *snake-stone* itself, I submitted one, the application of which I have been describing, to Mr. Faraday, and he has communicated to me, as the result of his analysis, his belief that it is "a piece of charred bone which has been filled with blood, perhaps several times, and then charred again." ......The probability is, that the animal charcoal, when instantaneously applied, may be sufficiently porous and absorbent to extract the venom from the recent wound together with a portion of the blood, before it has had time to be carried into the system......'—Tennent, *Ceylon*, I, 197-200.

(2) *Natural snake-stone.*—Tavernier, judging from the quotation already given, seems to doubt the existence of natural snake-stones, and credits the Brahmans with the pious fraud of their manufacture. Yet, in the following passage which immediately follows the earlier quotation, he describes, under the name

" stone of the hooded snake ", what we cannot distinguish from a natural snake-stone :

'There is still another stone,' continues Tavernier, 'which is called "stone of the hooded snake." It is a kind of snake which has, as it were, a hood which hangs behind the head, and it is behind this hood that the stone is found, the smallest being of the size of a hen's egg. There are snakes in Africa and in Asia of an enormous size, and up to 25 feet in length, as was that one whose skin is preserved at Batavia. This snake had swallowed a girl of eighteen years, of which fact I have elsewhere given an account. You find these stones only in snakes which are, at the least, two feet in length. The stone, which is not hard, when rubbed against another stone yields a kind of slime which, when dissolved in water and drunk by a person who has some poison in his body, has the property of driving it out at once. These snakes are only to be found on the coasts of Melinda, and you can obtain the stones from Portuguese sailors and soldiers on their return from Mozambique' (Tavernier, II, 121).

The snake-stone described by Dr. Davy (already quoted) may be a natural one.

Under the year 1772 *Hobson-Jobson* has a quotation from Thunberg, *Travels,* which is also worth reproducing: 'Being returned to Roode-Zand, the much celebrated *Snake-stone* (*Slangesteen*) was shown to me, which few of the farmers here could afford to purchase, it being sold at a high price, and held in great esteem. It is imported from the *Indies*, especially from Malabar, and cost several, frequently 10 or 12, rix dollars. It is round, and convex on one side, of a black colour, with a pale ash-grey speck in the middle, and tubulated with very minute pores......When it is applied to any part that has been bitten by a serpent, it sticks fast to the wound, and extracts the poison; as soon as it is saturated, it falls off of itself' (*Hobson-Jobson*, 848). We are unable to judge whether this is a natural or an artificial stone.

To the foregoing reports we can add two more opinions: Lt.-Col. T. Lewin (*A Fly on the Wheel*, 91-92), after recording a cure which was effected in his presence, says, 'I was thus effectually convinced that snake-charming is a real art, and not merely clever conjuring, as I had previously imagined. These so-called *snake-stones* are well known throughout India' (*Hobson-Jobson*, 848*b*). We are not told in this case if the stone was a natural or an artificial one. On the other hand, Patrick Russell has no faith in the curative qualities of a snake-stone (*Account of Indian Serpents*, 77); and Fayrer, speaking of snake-stones (*Thanatophidia of India*, 38 and 40), says (without distinguishing between natural and artificial ones) that 'a belief in their efficacy is a dangerous delusion' (*Hobson-Jobson*, 849*a*).

Muzaffar Ḥusain Mīrzā came from Kandahar to the Mughul court on 5 *Shahriwar*, XL R. Y. Among the presents he offered were 100 *'Irāqi* horses and a wonderful *muhra* (snake-stone), which when rubbed on a snake-bite became active and sucked out the poison, curing the patient.[1]

(5) *YADATASH* OR RAIN-STONE

According to the *Farhang-i-Anandrāj*, it was a stone which, when incantations were recited

---

[1] *A.N.*, III, 671; Tr., III, 1030. I have given my own translation.

over it, and the stone placed on the hand and put up to the sky, was believed to bring clouds and rain in abundance. This belief was widely current among the Turks. It is to be traced to the following incident in sacred history, which, however, is not to be found in the *Old Testament*.

It is related that when Japheth got leave from his father Noah, to proceed towards the east and the north with his family and relations, he requested his father to teach him a prayer which should bring rain whenever he wished it. The patriarch Noah gave him a stone which had that virtue, and either recited, or made a show of reciting, the *ism-i-a'ẓam* over it (*Akbarnāma*, I, 58). According to another version, Noah taught him the *ism-i-a'ẓam* and traced it on the stone (*Shajrat ul Atrak*. 24).

Japheth then set out on his journey, and produced rain with the help of that stone whenever he required it.

'It is said that this secret was disclosed to Noah by Gabriel, and that he was instructed, when he wanted rain, to repeat the name of God, to breathe on the stone, and throw it in water, and rain would then fall' (*Shajrat ul Atrak*, 24).

On Japheth's death the stone passed to his eldest son, Turk, who succeeded him.

This, we should remember, was the first stone of its kind.

This stone, which was called *jada-tāsh* or *yada-tāsh* by the Turks, *sang-i-yada* by the Persians, and *ḥajaru'l-maṭar* by the Arabs, was reported to be common among the Turks in later times—which presumably means that a *kind* of stone came in succeeding ages to be credited with similar properties, and was supposed to be descended in some mysterious way from the celebrated stone of Noah (*Akbar-nāma*, I, 58 ; *Shajrat ul Atrak*, 24).

Later on, the *yada*-stone was believed to bring not only clouds, wind and rain, but hail, snow, excessive cold and violent tempests.

An instance where the stone was merely thrown into water, and snow and hail appeared is cited in *Shajrat ul Atrak* on p. 66.

Another instance: When Tūlī Khān, son of Chingīz Khān, during the Mughuls' invasion of China in 627 *A.H.* (=1230 *A.C.*), was driven by the Chinese to Khaṭā, and was reduced to an extremity, he used the *sang-i-yada*, which brought snow and rain and intense cold. He thus scored a victory and put a large number of the enemy to the sword, taking some prisoner (Ghiāṣu'd-Dīn "Khwānd Mīr," *Ḥabību's-Siyar*, Bombay, 1857, III, Pt. i, 29).

Bābur often speaks of this stone in his *Memoirs*; and mention of it in Mughul history is frequent.

Abū'l-Faẓl, while describing Lār in the *sarkār* of Kashmir, speaks of a large lake on the mountain. 'If the flesh of an animal fall into it,' he says, 'a heavy fall of snow and rain ensues.'[1]

Rain-making with this stone, however, was not a common thing within the power of every tiro. It was an esoteric art and was practised

---

[1] *Ā'īn*, I, 569; Jarrett, II, 363-64.

professionally. Those who knew the use of the stone were called *yadahi* or *jadahi*.

The following paragraph is quoted from Leyden and Erskine's interesting note in the Introduction to their *Memoirs of Bābur*: 'Izzet-ullah,......in giving a description of Yārkand, mentions the *yadeh*-stone as on of the wonders of the land. He says that it is taken from the head of a horse or cow; and that, if certain ceremonies be previously used, it inevitably produces rain or snow. He who performs the ceremonies is called *yadehchī*. Izzet-ullah, though, like Bābur, he professes his belief in the virtues of the stone, yet acknowledges that he was never an eyewitness of its effects; he says, however, that he has so often heard the facts concerning its virtues stated over and over again, by men of unimpeachable credit, that he cannot help acquiescing in their evidence. When about to operate, the *yadehchi*, of whom there are many at this day in Yārkand, steeps the stone in the blood of some animal, and then throws it into water, at the same time repeating certain mysterious words. First of all, a wind is felt blowing, and this is soon succeeded by a fall of snow and rain. The author, aware of the incredulity of his readers, attempts to show that, though these effects certainly follow in the cold country of Yārkand, we are not to look for them in the warm region of Hind; and, further, ingeniously justifies his opinions regarding the unknown and singular qualities of the rain-stone by the equally singular and inexplicable properties of the magnet."[1]

Rai Anand Rām "Mukhlis" reports that a Turk, who understood the art of the *yada*-stone, was once on a visit to Nawwāb "Saifu'd-Daula" 'Abdu'ṣ-Ṣamad Khān, who was *Nāẓim* of Multān in the reign of Muḥammad Shāh. At the Nawwāb's request he gave the performance once, and produced plenty of cloud, and rain and hail.

The Emperor Muḥammad Shāh, having heard of it, directed his immediate attendance at Delhi; but by the time the orders reached Multān, the Turk had left for Turkistān, his home (*Mir'ātu'l-Iṣṭil* , P.U.L. MS., f. 136*b*).

---

[1] *Memoirs of Bābur*, tr. Leyden, Erskine and King, Introduction, pp. xci-xcii.

The *Shajrat ul Atrak* wrongly identifies this stone with, or at least assimilates it to, the bezoar-stone, and thus has misled many European scholars of repute. *Hobson-Jobson* (p. 445*a*) and *Tārikh-i-Rashīdi* (Engl. Tr., 32, f. n. 4 (p. 33) are examples. Nor is the word *jada* connected with jade (see *Hobson-Jobson*, *ibid.*).

The reader , who is interested in the question, and wants further information, is referred to a comprehensive note on the subject by Mr. Hodivala,[1] where the superstition is traced from Budhist times to quite a recent date.

(6) PHILOSOPHERS' STONE

Talking of stones, we might as well mention the philosophers' stone—the dream of the alchemist—of which just one record is available : While speaking of the buildings at Māndū, Jahāñgīr relates a story of how this stone was once found, used for a long time, and then lost. The naturalist-emperor cannot be expected to believe in such twaddle. Just as

---

[1] *Studies in Indo-Muslim History,* 134-36.

he gives the story for all it is worth, so do we his account—and his personal opinion:

'They say that before the time of Rāja Bikramājīt there was a Raja of the name of Jai Singh Deo. In his time a man had gone into the fields to bring grass. While he was cutting it, the sickle he had in his hand appeared to be of the colour of gold. When he saw that his sickle had been transmuted, he took it to a blacksmith of the name of Mādan [Māndan] to be repaired. The blacksmith knew the sickle had been turned into gold. It had before this been heard that there was in this country the alchemist's stone (*sang-i-pāras*), by contact with which iron and copper became gold. He immediately took the grass-cutter with him to that place and procured the stone. After this he brought to the Raja of the time this priceless jewel. The Raja by means of this stone made gold, and spent part of it on the buildings of this fort and completed them in the space of twelve years. At the desire of that blacksmith he caused them to cut into the shape of an anvil most of the stones that were to be built into the wall of the fort.

At the end of his life, when his heart had given up the world, he held an assembly on the bank of the Narbada, which is an object of worship among the Hindus, and, assembling brahmins, made presents to each of cash and jewels. When the turn of a brahmin came who had long been associated with him, he gave this stone into his hand. He from ignorance became angry and threw the priceless jewel into the river. After he came to know the true state of the affair he was a captive to perpetual sorrow. However much he searched, no trace of it was found. These things are not written in a book; they have been heard, but my intelligence in no way accepts this story. It appears to me to be all delusion.'[1]

Jahāñgīr, however, is not right in saying that the legend is not in the written book. In fact he seems to have taken it almost verbatim from *Ā'īn* (Text, I, 456; Jarrett, II, 197). Considering his relations with Abū'l-Fazl, one would not expect the emperor to acknowledge his source.

---

[1] *Tūzuk*, 180; R. & B., I, 364-65.

CHAPTER V

THE ACTUAL CONTENTS OF THE JEWEL TREASURY FROM THE INVASION OF BĀBUR TO THAT OF NĀDIR SHĀH

CHAPTER V

THE ACTUAL CONTENTS OF THE JEWEL TREASURY FROM THE INVASION OF BĀBUR TO THAT OF NĀDIR SHĀH

Now that we have surveyed the historical notices of precious and semi-precious stones and other valuable substances, we are in a position to try and form an idea of the actual amount of the total treasure; for while fragments, diarists' entries and anecdotes may be good history, they fail to produce an *impression* unless they are synthesized into a concrete and self-sustaining whole, and visualized as such.

It is as if after witnessing the presentations in court and other individual accretions to the Treasury we were now entering the Treasury itself, and trying to take stock of the wealth that has accumulated there.

The Indian Mughuls had a great reputation for wealth, which, as far as the Jewel Treasury is concerned, was well deserved. While the contents of the Cash Treasury waxed and waned with the exigencies of the Mughul Empire and with the habits and temperament of the Emperor, the Jewel Treasury grew without abatement, at least from the accession of Akbar down to Nādir Shāh's invasion in 1739.

The impressions of foreign travellers can be gathered from the following excerpts :

'Of these precious stones the Mogul has a quantity inherited from Taimūr-i-lang and the other kings, his predecessors, also those obtained in the conquests of the Bījāpur and Gulkandah kingdoms. In addition there are those he is daily buying. This takes no account of the fact that in these days he has become master of the diamond mines, and there is no stint of stones, the largest and best. For, although King Humāyūn was dethroned and expelled from his kingdom by Sher Shāh, he did not thereby lose his jewels, for he took them away and brought them back with him' (*Storia*, II, 343).

We are not sure about the 'Mogul' inheriting precious stones 'from Taimūr-i-lang.' Nor is any importance to be attached to the last sentence, which stands unsupported by any evidence.[1]

The following is more sensible: '*Chah-Jehan*,' says Bernier, 'who was a great economist, and reigned more than forty years without being involved in any great wars, never amassed six *kourours* of *roupies*.[2] But I do not include in this sum a great abundance of gold and silver articles, of various descriptions, curiously wrought, and covered with precious stones; or a prodigious quantity of pearls and gems of all kinds, of great size and value. I doubt whether any other Monarch possesses more of this species of wealth; a throne of the great *Mogol*, covered with pearls and diamonds, being alone valued, if my memory be correct,

---

[1] See below, pp. 509-14.

[2] A remark already dealt with under "Cash Treasury."

at three *kourours* of *roupies.*[1] But all these precious stones, and valuable articles, are the spoils of ancient princes, *Patans* and *Rajas*, collected during a long course of years, and increasing regularly under every reign, by presents which the *Omrahs* are compelled to make on certain annual festivals' (P. 223).

But this is only by way of introduction.

It is now time we attempted some stock-taking of the Mughul Jewel Treasury. We should love to have before us an authentic report of the contents of the Treasury for each of the major reigns, duly signed and verified by the Treasurer in charge at the time, setting forth, as was the rule, the number and the weight of the stones and pearls with the quality and the value of each clearly indicated. Unfortunately such a report, extremely desirable as it would be, is not available. But we possess a few documents of comparatively minor importance with which we shall have to shift as best we may. But we must begin at the beginning.

---

[1] For criticism of this, see Author's *Thrones, Chairs and Seats.*

BĀBUR

The swingeing victory of Panipat placed at Bābur's disposal the cumulated 'treasures of five kings.'[1] We have no doubt that huge quantities of jewels fell into Bābur's hands at Delhi and Agra, but we know also that Bābur showered money and jewels recklessly on his followers—princes, nobles, soldiers and the rest —just as he squandered the cash hoarded for generations by a line of thrifty kings before him. Some idea of the scale of munificence can be gathered from the following, which is only a part of the general distribution, which chances to be recorded :

Khwāja Kalān Beg repeatedly asked for leave to proceed to Kābul, as the climate of India did not suit him.

Bābur reluctantly gave him permission and by his hands sent the following presents for his relations at Kābul, with the instruction that all begums should set up their various tents in the garden of the audience-chamber, celebrate the occasion properly and thank God for the great

---

1 *Humāyūn Nāma*, 12.

victory, accepting these presents from the Emperor.

To each begum was to be presented one of Sultān Ibrāhīm's special dancing girls with a gold plate full of jewels—ruby, pearl, cornelian, diamond, emerald, turquoise, topaz and cat's-eye—two small mother-of-pearl trays full of *ashrafis* and two other trays full of *shāhrukhis* and all kinds of stuffs in sets of nine—four trays and one plate in all. And to the elder relations were sent a dancing girl, a plate of jewels, and a tray each of *ashrafis* and *shāhrukhis*—the dancing girl with the plate to be presented first, and the rest later. Jewels, *ashrafis*, *shāhrukhis* and stuffs were to be given to sisters, children, harams, kinsmen, begums, *āghās*, nurses, foster-brothers, *āghāchas* and others.

These instructions were carried out, and there were great doings for three days in the audience-hall garden at Kābul.[1]

---

[1] *Humāyūn Nāma*, 12-13. I have here freely translated, and slightly condensed, the passage, as a literal translation does not read well in English.

HUMĀYŪN

Humāyūn apparently carried about with him in his wanderings as many of the jewels as he could remove from the Jewel Treasury.

We do not hear much of them, however. On his way to Persia, near Bābā Ḥājī fort (in the south of Afghanistan), Humāyūn offered a ruby, a pearl and a few things to a Balūch chief, who had treated him kindly and shown devotion.[1]

Abū'l-Faẓl has already told us how after his arrival in Persia Humāyūn offered to Shāh Ṭahmāsp Bābur's famous diamond with 250 rubies.[2]

Gulbadan Begum has a different story to tell of the presentation of the jewels to the Shāh. She tells us that Humāyūn kept his collection of precious stones in a purse or pocket-book which he carried on his person, and which he left in charge of Hamīda Bānū Begum when he went out. The existence of

---

[1] *Humāyūn Nāma*, 68 [168].

[2] See p. 186 above.

it was known to none other than those two. One day the Begum went for a bath, and, wrapping up the purse in a handkerchief, put it on the Emperor's bed. Raushan Kūka, finding his opportunity, abstracted five rubies from the purse. He made common cause with Khwāja Ghāzī, another traitor, entrusted the rubies to him, and the two together made plans for their disposal. They went to a horse-coper and bought *tupchāq* horses for themselves, promising them the rubies in consideration.

When the Begum returned from the bath, the Emperor handed her the purse. Finding it too light, she at once suspected foul play and spoke to her husband. They were alarmed. The Begum acted promptly, took her brother, Khwāja Mu'azzam, into her confidence and asked him to make inquiry into the matter without making fuss. Khwāja Mu'azzam acted silently and skilfully. He interrogated the horse-merchants and Khwāja Ghāzī's servant, with the result that the little plot was discovered and the rubies located. Ultimately the rubies were tactfully recovered from Khwāja Ghāzī and restored to the Emperor.

Khwāja Ghāzī and Raushan Kūka, thus balked and disgraced, could think of no better plan of avenging themselves than carrying tales to the Shāh, and trying to poison his mind against their master. The Emperor noticed that the Shāh's manner towards him cooled and there were signs of estrangement. Humāyūn 'at once sent to the Shāh all the rubies and jewels that he possessed',[1] and explained the whole matter. The Shāh then admitted that Khwāja Ghāzī and Raushan Kūka were entirely responsible for the strained relations. The old cordiality was then restored, and the two mischiefmongers were handed over by Humāyūn to the Shāh, who cast them into prison (*Humāyūn Nāma*, 70-73).

As this is the only occasion on which presentation of jewels is mentioned in *Humāyūn Nāma*, this must be the great presentation including 'Bābur's diamond'. So thinks also Mrs. Beveridge (Tr., 173, f.n. 1).

---

[1] Mrs. Beveridge's rendering is not sufficiently clear on this point.

This story is only partially corroborated by Jauhar in the following passages. He writes: Humāyūn always carried 'his valuable diamonds and rubies in a purse in his pocket; but when he was performing his ablutions he generally laid them on one side; he had done so this day, and forgot them: it so happened that when the King was gone, and the humble servant *Jouher* was about to remount his horse, he saw a green-flowered purse lying on the ground, and a pen-case by the side of it: he immediately took them up, and as soon as he had overtaken the King, presented them'. Humāyūn was much astonished when he saw them, and was delighted (Stewart, 66-67; *Tazkara*, P.U.L. MS., f. 56*b*). Then he goes on to say that Humāyūn kept these valuables about him because he had formerly entrusted them to Raushan Beg, who had been guilty of dishonesty (Stewart, 67; *Tazkara*, f. 56*b*). This last is at variance with the version in *Humāyūn Nama*. Probably the facts of the matter did not come to Jauhar's knowledge, and when Jauhar heard that Raushan Kūka had stolen the jewels he thought he had been in charge of them.

The fullest account of the presentation of the jewels to the Shāh that we possess is found in the following passage in Jauhar :—' We remained several days encamped on the hunting grounds ; during this time his Majesty ordered his diamonds and rubies to be brought to him ; and having selected the largest diamond, placed it in a mother-of-pearl box ; he then added several other diamonds[1] and rubies ; and having placed them on a tray, gave them in charge of Byram Beg to present them to the Persian monarch, with a message, " that they were brought from Hindūstān purposely for his Majesty."

When Shāh Tahmāsp saw these precious stones he was astonished, and sent for his jewellers to value them. The jewellers declared they were above all price ; on which the Persian signified his acceptance, and conferred on Byram Beg the title of *khān*, with permission to use the kettle-drum and standard.[2] The diploma and insignia were sent the next

---

1 The MS. does not mention diamonds here.

2 No 'standard' in the MS.

day; but from that time, for two months, there was no intercourse of any kind between the monarchs' (Stewart, 68; *Tazkara*, f. 57 *a:b*). The last statement is cryptic. Probably Jauhar is thinking of the coolness caused by Raushan Kūka's backbiting, and has got mixed up about the time and the occasion.

Jauhar's account also refers to the great presentation. Major Stewart thinks the same (P. 68, f.n.). Excepting the slight discrepancies already noticed, there is nothing really inconsistent in the accounts of Gulbadan Begum and Jauhar. The reader has no doubt noticed that Raushan Kūka's episode occurred some time before Jauhar found the purse, and the presentation followed some days later.

AKBAR

We are emerging into daylight as we approach the reign of Akbar. Thanks to Abū'l-Fazl's encyclopaedic mind and method, we have some definite information about the contents of the Mughul Treasury, their arrangement and valuation. Akbar's great minister thus outlines the establishment of the Jewel Treasury and the method of classification and storing followed :

A treasurer, a clerk (*bitikchi*), a *dārogha* and a few experienced jewellers constituted the staff of the Treasury. The jewels were classified according to value in an elaborate system. Rubies were put in twelve classes, diamonds, emeralds, and red and blue *yāqūts* also in twelve classes, and pearls in sixteen.

The value of the rubies in each class ran as follows :

Class	Value					
1	From	1,000	*muhrs*		upwards	
2	,,	999	,,	to	500	*muhrs*
3	,,	499	,,	,,	300	,,
4	,,	299	,,	,,	200	,,
5	,,	199	,,	,,	100	,,
6	,,	99	,,	,,	60	,,
7	,,	59	,,	,,	40	,,
8	,,	39	,,	,,	30	,,
9	,,	29	,,	,,	10	,,
10	,,	9¾	,,	,,	5	,,
11	,,	4¾	,,	,,	1	*muhr*
12	,,	¾	*muhr*	,,	¼	rupee

The diamonds, emeralds, and red and blue *yāqūts* were likewise classified thus :—

Class	Value					
1	From	30	*muhrs*		upwards	
2	,,	29¾	,,	to	15	*muhrs*
3	,,	14¾	,,	,,	12	,,
4	,,	11¾	,,	,,	10	,,
5	,,	9¾	,,	,,	7	,,
6	,,	6¾	,,	,,	5	,,
7	,,	4¾	,,	,,	3	,,
8	,,	2¾	,,	,,	2	,,
9	,,	1¾	,,	,,	1	*muhr*
10	,,	A quarter rupee less than a *muhr*.		,,	5	rupees
11	,,	4¾	rupees	,,	2	,,
12	,,	1¾	,,	,,	¼	rupee

We don't know the weight of the stones assigned to the various classes either in this or in the previous list ; but the reader will see that while rubies ranging in price from 30 to 1000 *muhrs* and upwards are classified under eight heads, diamonds, emeralds and *yāqūts* of the same prices are all grouped together in the first class. In other words, rubies of *over*

30 *muhrs* and diamonds and other stones of *under* 30 *muhrs* are elaborately classified. From this one would be inclined to think that rubies or at least the high class ones, were, weight for weight, more valuable than other stones. But this is not true, for we learn a little lower down that a diamond worth 1 lakh of rupees weighed less than half as much as a ruby of the same price; though emeralds were several degrees cheaper than either.[1]

Pearls had sixteen classes :

Class	Value					
1	From	30	*muhrs*	upwards.		
2	,,	29¾	,,	to	15	*muhrs*
3	,,	14¾	,,	,,	12	,,
4	,,	11¾	,,	,,	10	,,
5	,,	9¾	,,	,,	7	,,
6	,,	6¾	,,	,,	5	,,
7	,,	4¾	,,	,,	3	,,
8	,,	2¾	,,	,,	2	,,
9	,,	1¾	,,	,,	1	*muhr*
10	From under	1	*muhr*	,,	5	rupees
11	,, ,,	5	rupees	,,	2	,,
12	,, ,,	2	,,	,,	1¼	,,
13	,, ,,	1¼	,,	,,	30	*dāms*
14	,, ,,	30	*dāms*	,,	20	,,
15	,, ,,	20	,,	,,	10	,,
16	,, ,,	10	,,	,,	5	,,

[1] See below.

The way these pearls were stored and strung is given in detail: Twenty pearls were placed on each of the strings in the first class. The actual number of the strings in this class is not given, since that probably varied from time to time. Next we are told that the total number of strings in each class corresponded to the class itself, *i.e.*, the second class contained two strings, the third class three strings, and the sixteenth class sixteen strings. In this case the number of pearls on each string is not known. Presumably it was kept elastic on purpose. This arrangement apparently did not apply to the first class, where the number of pearls on each string was fixed, and the total number of strings was left undetermined. The reader observes that in both cases room was left for fresh acquisitions and disbursements.

At the end of every string the royal seal was affixed, to guard against replacement or fraud.

Abū'l-Fazl then goes on to detail the charges for boring pearls, which varied with the class of the pearl bored.

Next follow the prices of jewels of unusual weight and value in Akbar's Treasury:

Kind of Jewel	Weight				Price
Ruby.	11	*tunk.*	20	*ratis*	Rs. 100,000
Diamond.	5	"	16	"	" 100,000
Emerald.	17	"	21	"	" 52,000
Yuqūt.	4	"	7¾	"	" 50,000
Pearl.	5	"	0	"	" 50,000

(*Āīn*, Text, I, 11-12; Blochmann, 15-16).

The weight and price of the ruby correspond beautifully to those of (1) a ruby purchased by Mahābat Khān from a European and offered to Jahāṅgīr (Jahāṅgīr's Reign, No. 15),[1] and (2) the engraved ruby sent by Shāh 'Abbās to Jahāṅgīr and ultimately set on the rail of the Peacock Throne (*Ibid.*, No. 22).[1]

As regards the value of diamonds, No. 10 of Jahāṅgīr's reign in our list[2] weighed less than 80 *ratis* and was valued at one lakh of

[1] Table I of Rubies on pp. 292-95.
[2] Table I of Diamonds on pp. 230-35.

rupees, while Nos. 1 and 2 of Shāh Jahān's reign (which may be one and the same stone) weighed 100 *ratis* each and were priced at one lakh likewise; whereas No. 3, which had the same weight, carried the price, 1,50,000 rupees. It thus appears that the prices of diamonds ruled much higher in the reigns of Jahāṅgīr and Shāh Jahān than in Akbar's time.

JAHĀṄGIR

As the reader is aware, we possess the De Laët-Manrique inventory of the treasure left by Akbar in 1605, the cash part of which was given and discussed in the chapter on 'Cash Treasury.' The remaining portion of it can now be set forth.

For convenience of treatment the inventory of the Jewel Treasury is given entire, although it comprises besides precious stones and gems, ornaments, furniture, gold and silver plate and utensils, statues, porcelain, books, cloths and woollens, tents and curtains, arms and accoutrements, harness and housings. These items will be severally treated of elsewhere.

But with the details of gems and jewels fresh in the reader's mind, I have considered it worth while to attempt an estimate of the entire contents of the Jewel Treasury at this stage, although it includes a great deal of miscellaneous wealth not usually counted as treasure. This course seems better than breaking up the lists into individual items, and distributing them over the various treatises dealing with those details. Nor would it be possible to discuss the value and utility of these lists if their contents were so dissipated. These considerations have led the writer to place this chapter on the 'Actual Contents of the Jewel Treasury' immediately after gems and jewels, the fuller details of many of the articles summarized here being reserved for future treatment.

Articles	Value in rupees
Diamonds, rubies, emeralds, sapphires, pearls, and similar gems. ..	60,520,521
Wrought gold, including necklaces. ..	19,006,745
Golden furniture (*supellex*); all kinds of gold plate; various images of elephants, horses, camels, and similar animals, made of gold. ..	9,507,992
Wrought silver, such as goblets (*scyphi*), dishes (*disci*), candlesticks, columns, and other vases and utensils of every kind. ..	2,225,838

Articles	Value in rupees
Brazen (*aenea*) vessels and furniture of every kind and fashion. ..	51,225
Most elegant vessels of every kind in porcelain (Manrique adds 'and also of coloured Glass,' *i.e.*, crystal). ..	2,507,747
Books written by great men, and adorned with extremely valuable bindings (24,000 volumes). ..	6,463,731
Cloths interwoven with gold and silver, from Persia, Turkey, Gujarāt, and Europe; also silks of various kinds; with cotton goods from Bengal and other provinces. ..	15,509,979
Woollen cloths, European, Persian, and Tartar. ..	503,252
Tents, hangings, umbrellas (*canopea*), rugs, and all things needed for the adornment of houses or for camp use. ..	9,925,545
Engines of war (*tormenta bellica*), mortars (*bombardae*), balls, and gunpowder—as well as other military material. ..	8,575,971
Weapons—shields, swords, daggers, bows, arrows, and the like. ..	7,555,525
Harness, bits of gold and silver, and everything else pertaining to horse furniture. ..	2,525,646
Housings decorated with gold and silver (*tunicae equestres*) [Mandelslo: 'covering-clothes for horses and elephants']; cloaks of every kind, and royal arms (*arma regalia*) ['Various kinds of coats and equestrian ornaments, worked and embroidered with gold, silver, and precious stones, including the arms borne and insignia carried before the Imperial person and those of the Royal house.'—Manrique]. ..	5,000,000
Total ..	149,879,717

De Laët, 108-9; Manrique, II, 293-94; Smith, *J.R.A.S.*, 1915, 241-42).

It is to be noticed that thrones and chairs are not specifically mentioned in De Laët's list. We must presume them to be included under 'Golden furniture (*supellex*).'

It is now fairly established that Manrique, who is much over-estimated by V. A. Smith, only copied out De Laët's list, so that his document has no independent—and at best only a corroborative—value. De Laët's *De Imperio Magni Mogolis* was published in 1631, while Manrique's *Itinerario* appeared in 1640. But these dates should not mislead us, as the two documents are only copies of the identical official record, which represented the state of things at the death of Akbar.

It may be noted in passing that in Mr. Hoyland's translation the amounts have been carelessly transcribed in one or two cases, though the total given by him tallies with the true total of the sums, showing that the former are only clerical errors. For this and other reasons I have considered it safe to adopt Smith's translation, which is made after collation of original texts, not entirely excluding even Mandelslo's, which he considers spurious.

This can be followed up with Hawkins' account of the contents of Jahāṅgīr's Treasury about 1610, when Hawkins was at the Mughul court.

Precious stones and pearls.	Weight or number.
Diamonds of not less than 2½ car., 'rough, of all sorts and sizes, great and small'. ..	1½ battmans or 82½ lb.
'Ballace rubies little and great, good and bad.' ..	2,000 pieces
Pearls of all sorts. ..	12 battmans or 660 lb.
Rubies of all sorts. ..	2 battmans or 110 lb.
Emeralds of all sorts. ..	5 battmans or 275 lb.
Yashm or jade, which comes from Cathay. ..	1 battman. or 55 lb.
Stones of Yemen [1](which is a red stone).	5,000 pieces.
All other sorts, such as corals, topaz, etc. ..	'An infinite number.'

Ornaments and Jewelled Gold and Silver Ware.	Number or weight.
Chains of pearls and chains of all sorts of precious stones. ..	'An infinite number.'
Rings 'with Jewels of rich Diamants, Ballace Rubies, Rubies and old Emerods'. ..	,,

[1] Probably *'aqīq* (cornelian or agate).

Ornaments and Jewelled Gold and Silver Ware.	Number or weight.
'Swords of Almaine Blades, with the Hilts and Scabberds set with divers sorts of rich stones, of the richest sort.' ..	2,200
Poniards of two sorts. ..	2,000
Saddle drums, used in hawking: very rich ones of gold, set with stones. ..	500
Brooches 'for their heads, where-into their Feathers be put': very rich. ..	2,000
Saddles of gold and silver set with stones. ..	1,000
Teukes (great lances) covered with gold, and the fluke (point) set with stones ('These instead of their colours, are carryed, when the King goeth to the warres'). ..	25
Kittasoles (umbrellas, *i.e.*, the *chatr*) of state. 'None in his Empire dareth in any sort have any of these carryed for his shadow but himselfe.'	20
Chairs of state (De Laët calls these thrones, and probably rightly) of silver 3, of gold 2 ..	5
Other chairs of silver and gold. ..	100
Rich glasses (*i.e.*, mirrors). ..	200
Vases for wine, 'very faire and rich, set with Jewels.' ..	100
Drinking cups (Fifty of these very rich, being 'made of one piece of Ballace Ruby, and also of Emerods, of Eshim, of Turkish stone, and of other sorts of stones'). ..	500
Plate (dishes, cups, basins, pots and beakers) of silver ..	2,000 battmans or 110,000 lb.
of gold ..	1,000 battmans or 55,000 lb.

Hawkins (Purchas, III, 32-33).

The thrones and chairs are all expressly included and separately enumerated in this list.

The reader will notice that although these two independent accounts refer to very nearly the same period, the dates being only five years apart, yet it is not possible for us to compare or verify the items; since De Laët gives only the total value of each set of articles in rupees, while Hawkins gives the total number of the articles, and sometimes their total weight.

For comparison or verification we have to fall back upon *Muntakhabu'l-Lubāb*. The reader has already seen that, according to Khāfī Khān, the Emperor's jewels (*jawāhir-i-khāṣṣa*), at Akbar's death, weighed one maund and were worth over three crores of rupees (*M. L.*, I, 243). Now De Laët places the total value of diamonds, rubies, emeralds, sapphires, pearls and other gems, at well over six crores, which is just about double Khāfī Khān's estimate. As for the weight, Hawkins gives weights for five gems out of eight in his list:

these total 21½ *battmans* or maunds. Counting in the other gems, at a guess, the total weight of precious and semi-precious stones and pearls would be over 30 maunds—as against one maund of Khāfī Khān. No reconciliation between these authorities is possible even by assuming that Khāfī Khān is counting only precious gems, and ignoring all semi-precious stuff; for diamonds, rubies, pearls and emeralds (in Hawkins' list) alone exceed 20 maunds, even leaving 'ballace rubies' out of account. The result is utter chaos. The present writer has more respect for the two inventories elaborately copied out by the European travellers than for Khāfī Khān's irresponsible statements.

SHĀH JAHĀN

Shāh Jahān's reign represents the heyday of material splendour and prosperity, and with his accession the art of collecting, valuing and classifying jewels entered on a new career. The leading spirit of the age, the Emperor himself, was a great connoisseur of pearls and stones.

Let us for a moment step backward to get a true perspective.

Vicissitudes had come to an end with Humāyūn, and the sledgehammer strokes of Akbar's victories gave a rough outline to an empire, which fifty years of wise and tolerant government was gradually to make shipshape and tolerably homogeneous.

The opportunities offered by the settled government and peace left behind by Akbar were not however used to the best advantage by his son. With all the advantages of a strong and healthy constitution, high education and a mind delicately responsive to the appeal of natural phenomena, he had a fine temperament, a healthy curiosity, highly developed tastes and an extensive range of interests. With all this to his credit, his intemperate habits, specially in the latter half of his reign, reduced him to the condition of a *roi fainéant*, the real power being vested in the hands of Nūr Jahān, who, considering her disabilities, steered the ship of state with remarkable ability and talent.

Against this background Shāh Jahān's accession stands out in conspicuous relief. The increasing resources of a peacefully progressing empire were at once placed at the disposal of a man who understood the true meaning and value of wealth—who did not spend a pice where no return was assured, and who did not scruple to spend millions where to his mind a real need was being satisfied.

Shāh Jahān had a great passion for art and a particularly well-balanced aesthetic judgment. His attachment to precious stones has often been misinterpreted as grasping cupidity, whereas, in point of fact, that emperor was the most liberal and the most generous in the whole line of Mughul kings, not only with his money but in his ideas and sympathies, his daily dealings and actions. Bernier describes him as a great economist. [1]

On whatever he has left us we see an indelible impress of unapproachable ideals and an unerring eye for effect. Designs and proportions of his buildings and gardens, quality

[1] P. 223.

and symmetry of their patterns and decorations, even furnishings of his halls and chambers, and dispositions and arrangements in his durbars, and finally the miracles of the jeweller's art—in all these we find a master mind trying to realize its dreams of beauty and perfection in terms of brick or stone here, of line and colour there, of gold and jewels and precious stuffs, using the costliest material with nonchalant ease and seemingly reckless extravagance. The noble band of designing architects, painters and jewellers played up to his ideas and plans in a way that does credit to all concerned.

We must not forget that both as prince and even after his deposition Shāh Jahān was considered a great connoisseur of pearls and precious stones. The reader remembers how Jahāṅgīr was once worried over finding a match for a pearl to put on an armlet, and Prince K͟hurram rootled out a beautiful one from an old disused *sar-pech* of Akbar's, which nobody knew of.[1] It shows that the Prince from a boy had an eagle's eye for jewels, and

---

[1] Pp. 270-72 above.

did not forget one when he had once seen it.

The reader will also remember the occasion when Aurangzeb and his court jewellers were puzzled by a ruby, and the question of its genuineness or otherwise was referred to S̱hāh Jahān in prison, as the greatest living authority on the subject, his verdict being accepted as final by all parties.[1]

Things being what they are, we approach this reign with high hopes and a whetted curiosity. But as far as the actual figures of treasury totals are concerned these hopes are doomed to be foiled. Unfortunately we do not possess any reasonably authentic catalogue of the contents of S̱hāh Jahān's Jewel Treasury.

Mandelslo, who came in 1638, has the following: 'I was credibly informed, that the *Mogul*, who lived in my time, had a Treasure, which amounted to above fifteen hundred Millions of Crowns' (P. 37): This appraisement of the total wealth at the end of the first decade

---

[1] See pp. 286-88 above.

comes to 300 crores of rupees. And this, even if it includes both cash and jewels (which probably it does), is, on the face of it, a gross exaggeration based on unverified rumours.

Again, after giving the inventory of Akbar's treasure, which is the De Laët-Manrique document, he continues: 'But this came not any thing near the Treasure which *Scach Choram* was possessed of, at the time of my Travels in those Parts. This Wealth is more and more augmented every day, not so much out of the ordinary Revenue coming in from the great Kingdoms he hath.................. as by the Presents which are made him, and the Escheats falling to him at the death of great Lords and Favourites' (P. 38). It is to be noted that this passage does not form part of the earlier German edition (1656) of Mandelslo's work, and is adjudged to be spurious by critics. But as Mr. Commissariat remarks, though these 'elaborate additions' 'are not from Mandelslo's pen, they have nevertheless a historical importance of their own, for the information given in them is based on the best books on eastern travels available to Olearius or to de Wicquefort in the middle of the seventeenth century.'[1]

For a more sober estimate we must resort to S͟hāh Jahān's court historian. Mulla 'Abdu'l-Ḥamīd of Lahore, after speaking (under XVIII R.Y.) of the *sar-pech* which consisted of five rubies and twenty-four pearls and was valued at 12 lakhs, and of the *tasbiḥ* comprising five rubies and thirty pearls, valued at 8 lakhs, and of two other *tasbiḥs* of pearls and *yaqūts* (total price, 20 lakhs),[2] goes on to say that although most of these gems have come down from Akbar's time, additions continued to be made during the reigns of Jahāṅgīr and S͟hāh Jahān, so that in this reign a wealth of gems and jewels has accumulated, to which the treasury of no other monarch in the world can present a parallel. The total value of this wealth, not counting 2 crores' worth of gems presented to princes and others during this reign, is 5 crores. Out of this total

---

[1] M. S. Commissariat, *Mandelslo's Travels in Western India (A.D. 1638-39)*, pp. xv-xvi.

[2] See pp. 281-84 above.

gems and jewelled articles to the value of 2 crores of rupees are worn on the Emperor's person, and are kept in charge of trustworthy servants in the *mahal*; and the remainder worth 3 crores is kept outside in charge of *chelas* (slaves) (*B. N.*, II, 391-93).[1]

After the earlier statement in the superlative these figures seem tame and read almost like an anti-climax. But both statements are accurate, and there is no attempt at creating an impression.

But in a reign like Shāh Jahān's, disbursements should also be taken into account. The same writer, when reviewing Shāh Jahān's cash treasure at the end of XX R.Y., remarks that since the beginning of this reign

---

1 Khāfī Khān says Shāh Jahān inherited 10 crores' worth of gems and jewelled things. Up to XVIII R.Y. 2 crores' worth had been given away in gifts and presents, and a half crore in charity (*ma'jūnāt*, *sadqa* and *nisār* on weighments and festivals), while the value of 5 crores was present in the Jewel Treasury at this date, the rest, worn on the Emperor's body, being in the *toshak khāna* among the royal wardrobe (*M.L.*, I, 605). Where this account agrees, or can be reconciled, with the authentic and explicit statement in *B.N.*, cited above, it is welcome, and where it differs it is to be received with caution.

Rs. 9,50,00,000 in cash and kind has been given away as *in'am*, nearly half in cash, and a little over half in articles.[1] These articles mean, besides horses, elephants, etc., gems, jewelled arms, housings, stuffs and the like, and came to some 5 crores in value. In view of the remark already quoted we can readily understand that this sum included the two crores' worth of pearls and stones given away to princes etc.

These no doubt include the gems and jewels given away on the following occasions, of which only a passing mention can be made here.

We know that from Shāh Jahān's Coronation (8 *Jumādā* II, 1037) to the end of the first Nauroz (beginning of *Sha'bān*)—in seven weeks odd—jewels, dresses and arms, and horses, elephants and cash to the value of 1,80,00,000 rupees were disbursed.[2] This included 76 lakhs' worth presented to Mumtāzu'z-Zamānī, the empress. Most of this wealth

---

[1] B. N., II, 713.

[2] *B.N.*, I, i, 192. Author's *History of Shāh Jahān's Reign*, Ch. iii.

must have reverted to the Treasury on her death. Deducting that amount from the total, we have well over a crore of rupees left. Half of this, we know definitely, was the price of jewellery presented to Jahān Ārā Begum and the princes. So out of this total we may assume some 60 lakhs to stand for gems and jewels.

Next we may notice the weddings of the first princes of the blood. The amount spent on Dārā Shukoh's marriage (1042 A.H.) on the Emperor's side was 22 lakhs of rupees, which included approximately some 10 lakhs' worth of gems and jewels,[1] and the expenditure on the occasion of Shāh Shujā''s wedding (same year) would be in the neighbourhood of 12 lakhs, half of which we may assume to be the price of jewels.[2] Similarly on the weddings of Aurangzeb[3] (end of 1046) and Murād Bakhsh[4] (1052 A. H.) the Emperor gave them Rs. 10 lakhs and 5 lakhs in cash respec-

---

[1] *B.N.*, I, i, 454 and 460 ; *A.S.*, I, 524.

[2] *B.N.*, I, i, 462 ; *A.S.*, I, 540.

[3] *B.N.*, I, ii, 267.

[4] *B.N.*, II, 304.

tively, to make the necessary purchases and arrangements. The total expenses therefore would come to some 20 lakhs for the two weddings, half or nearly half of it being represented by the price of gems.

Another large item we can notice is the ornaments and jewelled articles worth 10 lakhs given away to Jahān Arā Begum and a similar value bestowed on princes, princesses and nobles at the time of the celebration of her recovery (*Shawwāl*, 1054 A.H.).[1] The latter amount included some cash and animals, so that it will be safer to place the jewels at some 7 lakhs out of this sum. The total value of gems disbursed on this occasion would thus come to some 17 lakhs of rupees.

This feast and the weddings thus account for some 40 lakhs, and with the 60 lakhs disbursed at the opening of the reign, would come to just a crore's value in jewels. But these are only a few of the outstanding items.

---

[1] *B.N.*, II, 397.

There was, throughout the reign, a stream of costly presents constantly flowing from the Emperor to the princes and nobles, and back again to the Emperor.

It must not be forgotten that we are considering the treasure as it existed at the end of the second decade of this reign. The third decade was perhaps the most prosperous in Mughul Indian history: a larger value in gems and jewels changed hands at the court of Delhi during the years 1648-58 than at any period of Indian history before or since.

Some rough indications can be gathered from the following facts: On the first durbar held in the newly-built Delhi palace, which fell on a Nauroz (Monday, 18 *Rab.* I, 1060, and following days) presents worth 15 lakhs were accepted. Again, the value accepted from princes and nobles in XXVIII R. Y. totalled nearly 15 lakhs[1] and that in XXIX R.Y. came to 20,[2] while in R.Y. XXX the maximum of nearly 1 crore was reached.[3]

[1] *B.N.*, III, P.U.L. MS., f. 99*a*.
[2] *B.N.*, III, P.U.L. MS., f. 108*a*.
[3] *B.N.*, III, P.U.L. MS., f. 123*b*.

Jewels of course only constituted a proportion of these figures, and yet a goodly proportion.

It is a pity that the total of the collection at the end of the reign is not recorded either by Muḥammad Wāris or by Muḥammad Ṣāliḥ, the prime contemporary authorities for this period. Nor is there available an estimate of total disbursements either during the third decade or during the whole reign.

All that we can offer the reader is the following : According to Khāfī Khān, Shāh Jahān left in the Treasury uncoined gold and silver, and gold and silver vessels and jewels worth 15 or 16 crores.[1] The price of bullion is not separately given, but, taking Khāfī Khān's account of Akbar's treasure[2] as our guide, and allowing for the higher price of gold at this date and for acquisitions in Shāh Jahān's reign, we can guess that it would be somewhere near 2 crores.

The items that go to make the remaining 14

[1] *M.L.*, I, 758, and p. 51 above.

[2] *M.L.*, I, 243 and Chapter on Cash Treasury above.

crores are not given, but this total of the treasure in 1658 comes so close to the De Laët-Manrique total for 1605 that we are tempted to square off the two, and declare that all these documents corroborate each other, and we have at last arrived at a reliable grand total of the Mughul jewel treasury.

But then we are assuming that the prosperity and resources of the Mughul empire were marking time during the palmiest half-century of its history—which is contrary to known facts. One is inclined to look for a great advance on the previous figures towards the latter end of Shāh Jahān's reign. Judging from the wording of Khāfī Khān's statement, one would confine his total to gold and silver vessels and gems and jewelled things, which he actually names, so that the value of such items as porcelain, books, stuffs, tents, weapons and housings, which are included by De Laët-Manrique, will have to be added to Khāfī Khān's estimate before we can place the two totals side by side. These latter come to nearly six crores, and should be well over 7 crores at the end of

Shāh Jahān's reign. This would bring the total value of Shāh Jahān's wealth (about the year 1658) to a figure in the neighbourhood of 23 crores, besides 24 crores of coined money. To this grand total of 47 crores is to be added some 3 crores, more or less, spent by that emperor on his programme of building operations; and another 5 crores as a rough valuation of animals and birds in the royal stables, menageries, aviaries, etc., and of carts, carriages, boats and similar articles, which were not costly enough to be included in the inventories already given.

This amount of 55 crores, measured in purchasing power, is equivalent to some 250 crores to-day, which compares very favourably with the gold reserve in the issue department of the Bank of England on November 2, 1927, which was 149·7 millions[1] or, roughly, just over 200 crores of rupees at £1 = Rs. 13-8 a.

---

[1] *Encyclopaedia Britannica,* III, 54.

For the actual contents of Aurangzeb's jewel treasury we have no official or non-official record to guide us. Of course we know that the priceless gems and rarities of the age, which Shāh Jahān's well-known discrimination and patronage attracted from far and near and which he sedulously gathered and cherished during thirty years of unexampled prosperity—all this and all that had descended to him from the times of Akbar and Jahāṅgir passed peacefully into Aurangzeb's hands.

To the inherited treasury Aurangzeb must have added considerably during the long reign of nearly fifty years, in which the frontiers of the empire were extended and the revenues increased. It is true that the royal patronage for this class of goods diminished in this period and the efforts for artistic creation missed the incentive they had received during the preceding three reigns; but it is also true that Aurangzeb was a thrifty and sound administrator and, although large cash gifts were frequent in his reign, he was not nearly so lavish of jewels as his father; so that we may be sure that the contents of the existing jewel treasury were sedulously guarded, while the customary stream of presents continued unabated to swell the total hoard. In particular, the conquest of Bījāpur and Golconda (in 1686-87) must have meant accession to the treasury.

This monarch inherited the major portion of his father's treasury at the time of his accession. But quite a large number of valuable items remained outside, and came in at subsequent dates.

Many costly jewels, arms and ornaments were bestowed on Dārā Shukoh on various occasions during Shāh Jahān's reign. The climax was reached when during the latter's fateful illness ornaments and jewelled arms and articles to the value of some 35 lakhs of rupees were bestowed on that prince on a single occasion (1068 *A. H.*).[1] The accretion of wealth in the hands of Dārā Shukoh by this time must have been immense.

---

[1] See below, and *B.N.*, III, 141*b*-142*a*.

Khāfī Khān states on the authority of an assistant *mushrif* of the Jewel Treasury, whom he describes as a 'reliable witness', that Dārā Shukoh, before the battle of Samūgarh, left jewels and pearls worth 27 lakhs of rupees belonging to the ladies of his haram[1] in the *mibal* jewel-house in Agra fort. Shāh Jahān was privy to it, but Dārā Shukoh, after his defeat, got no time in his precipitate flight to get possession of them. Aurangzeb came to know of it and insisted on the restoration of the valuables to the Treasury. After some unpleasantness between father and son, Shāh Jahān had to surrender them; and, what is more, the messenger who carried them to Aurangzeb was also the bearer of the deposed monarch's letter pardoning Aurangzeb for his undutiful conduct. Khāfī Khān quotes in full Aurangzeb's letter acknowledging the "pardon" and the gift (*M. L.*, II, 104-6).

At the time of the battle at Deorāi (near Ajmīr) we catch a glimpse of Dārā Shukoh's

[1] In an earlier part of the passage the author describes them as belonging to Dārā Shukoh's dress (p. 104).

treasure, and gold and silver vessels and other movables loaded on elephants, camels and horses, with ladies of his haram on elephants,[1] all left under a guard of cavalry and infantry on the banks of the Anā Sāgar tank near Ajmīr (*'Ālamgīrnāma*, 409). Much of this was plundered by the guards themselves after the defeat of the unfortunate prince (*Ibid.*, 410).[1]

Most of Dārā Shukoh's jewels probably found their way into the state treasury sooner or later. Aurangzeb appropriated them, says Tavernier, 'after he had caused his [Dārā Shukoh's] head to be cut off' (I, 317).

Shāh Shujā' also had his collection of valuables, which he carried about with him in his adversity and wanderings. On 7 *Muḥarram*, 1071, Ikhlāṣ Khān Khweshgī brought to court his ladies, cash and jewel treasure, and other goods (*'Ālamgīrnāma*, 573).

Jahān Ārā Begum was Shāh Jahān's favourite daughter and had been constantly receiving presents during the thirty years of her father's illustrious reign. She must have built up

[1] See also *M.L.*, II, 72-73 and 80-81.

quite a tidy collection of valuables, which remained with her during her self-imposed incarceration with her father.

Towards the end of 1070 Jahān Ārā Begum paid a visit to Aurangzeb and offered a string of pearls and 5 rubies worth Rs. 2,80,000 ('*Ālamgīrnāma*, 568); and again sent some jewels and jewelled articles to him in *Shawwāl*, 1072 (*Ibid.*, 743).

Tavernier, talking apparently of the course of events before Aurangzeb's coronation, remarks nonchalantly that Aurangzeb 'took possession of all the wealth which she [Begum Ṣāḥib] had received from her father's liberality' (I, 274). But only on the next page, where the author is speaking of the happenings immediately after Shāh Jahān's death, we read, 'The Begam Sāhib also had a quantity of precious stones, which he had not taken from her when he placed her in the fortress, as he was then satisfied with securing the gold and silver with which her chests were full' (P. 275). So 'all the wealth' in the first passage does not include the 'quantity of precious stones' in the second. Tavernier's vague and inexact ways of talking do not enable us to feel any confidence even where he makes a perfectly definite and precise statement. The reader doubtless remembers the many occasions, on which this author has been judged and found wanting.

Bernier's remark is entitled to more respect, though it does not carry us far: He tells us that when, after the death of Shāh Jahān, Aurangzeb visited Agra fort, Jahān Ārā Begum received him with much courtesy and 'presented him with a large golden basin, full of precious stones—her own jewels, and those which belonged to *Chah-Jehan*' (P. 199). This may, and probably does, refer to only a small proportion of the treasure which had been in possession of the late emperor and his daughter.

As for the division of Jahān Ārā Begum's belongings after her death Manucci has the following: 'At the time of her death this princess divided her property and jewels among her nieces, leaving to each a good deal of money and jewels. Nor did she overlook her beloved Jānī Begam, to whom she bequeathed her finest jewels and a greater share of money' (*Storia*, II, 256).

Now we come to the gems and jewels in Shāh Jahān's possession in Agra fort.

We know that Shāh Jahān sent to Aurangzeb (1 *Rajab*, 1072) jewels to the value of 16 lakhs by the hands of Fāẓil Khān, *Mīr Sāmān*, who had been sent to Agra (presumably for the purpose) by Aurangzeb a month earlier (*'Ālamgīrnāmā*, 660-62; *M.L.*, II, 129-30). It is possible that these were the precious stones mentioned by Bernier (on p. 166) in the passage quoted below.

Khāfī Khān reports that Shāh Jahān had a rosary of 100 round pearls all of the same colour and weight, which was worth 4 lakhs of rupees. The pearls had been got together after much care and research. Besides there was an *ārsī*[1] of diamond which he always wore round his neck. Aurangzeb sent a

[1] An *ārsi*, as we know it today in India, is a ladies' thumb-ring set with a small mirror. We hope there is no misprint in the text.

eunuch with the message asking for these ornaments. The aged monarch was furious: he gave away the *ārsi*, but concerning the rosary sent back the reply that it was used in his devotions, and it could only be surrendered after it had been pounded in a mortar. It was never asked for again (*M. L.*, II, 106-7). This reminds us of the following passage in Bernier, though it refers apparently to a different occasion.

Aurangzeb once asked his father for some precious stones, which he wanted, he said, to complete a piece of workmanship that he was adding to the peacock throne. 'The captive Monarch indignantly answered that *Aureng-Zebe* should be careful only to govern the kingdom with more wisdom and equity: he commanded him not to meddle with the throne; and declared that he would be no more plagued about these jewels, for that hammers were provided to beat them into powder the next time he should be importuned upon the subject' (Bernier, 127).

But later, we are informed, the relations

between father and son improved. Aurangzeb paid the aged monarch every attention, indulged all his wishes, and afforded him every facility consistent with close confinement. 'Indeed, *Aureng-Zebè's* behaviour was throughout kind and respectful, and he paid attention to his aged parent in every possible way. He loaded him with presents, consulted him as an oracle, and the frequent letters of the son to the father were expressive of duty and submission. By these means *Chah-Jehan's* anger and haughtiness were at length subdued, insomuch that he frequently wrote to *Aureng-Zebe* on political affairs, sent *Dara's* daughter to him, and begged his acceptance of some of those precious stones, which he had threatened to grind to powder if again importuned to resign them' (*Ibid.*, P. 166).

Tavernier has a different version of this matter: Aurangzeb begged S͟hāh Jahān, 'as he was about to ascend the throne in a few days, to have the kindness to send some of his jewels to be used on that day, so that he might appear before his people with the same magnificence as the other Emperors, his predecessors, had done. Shāh Jahān became so enraged at this demand of Aurangzeb, which he regarded as an insult levelled at him in his prison by his son, that for some days he was like a madman, and he even nearly died. In the excess of his passion he frequently called for a pestle and mortar, saying that he would pound up all his precious stones and pearls, so that Aurangzeb might never possess them. But the Begam Sāhib, his eldest daughter, who had never left him, threw herself at his feet, and besought him not to proceed to such an extremity, and as she had full power over him in consequence of the intimate relations which existed between them[1], she appeased him, rather with the object of keeping the precious stones for herself than to give pleasure to her brother, her mortal enemy who might one day become their possessor. Thus, when Aurangzeb ascended the throne he had only one jewel on his cap (*toque*); but if he had desired more he did not lack them, as I have elsewhere said, and he asked for the stones from his father only with the intention of retaining them permanently' (295-96).

---

[1] An unwarranted libel.

Probably every statement in the latter half of this passage is historically incorrect. From the points common to the two accounts we are disposed to think that the passages already cited from Bernier constitute an accurate record of events as they occurred, and Tavernier has mistaken the occasion on which the dispute took place, and mixed up things in general. Knowing Tavernier as we do, this is not surprising.

Of course we could guess that all valuables which remained with the imprisoned monarch were, on his death, restored to Aurangzeb's Treasury, even if Tavernier did not tell us, as he does, that 'as soon as Aurangzeb had news of it [his father's death] he came to Agra and seized all the jewels of the late King, his father, which he had not secured during his life' (I, 275).

Although we possess no inventory of Aurangzeb's Jewel Treasury, we happen to have a somewhat detailed list of the Delhi treasure plundered by Nādir S̲h̲āh. Nādir's invasion came only 32 years after the death of

Aurangzeb, and nobody will think that any appreciable addition was made to the store during those years. So the quantity and value of Nādir's plunder may be safely taken as the measure of the treasure left by Aurangzeb.

The following passages from James Fraser's *History of Nadir Shah* are extremely interesting:

'*Nadir Shah*, after his Victory, and having established his Power, had demanded of *Nizam al Muluck*, twenty *Crore* [1] of *Rupees* (exclusive of the Jewels, Gold Plate set with precious Stones, and other fine Goods, seized of the King's, and other *Omras*) to be collected in the best Manner he could out of the King's Treasury, his own Effects, and all the other *Omras*, wealthy People and Inhabitants. Such a Sum was not to be raised out of the King's Treasury, or the *Omras* Effects; for, in the King's, the Gold and Silver Coins did not exceed three Crore:[2] But, in the inward Vaults (which had been shut up and sealed for many Years, no Body knowing by whom they

[1] 'Twenty *Crores* are 25 millions Sterling' (Footnote).
[2] '3,750,000 *l*' (Footnote).

were sealed, or what they contained) there was found of Gold and Silver to a much larger Amount than the Money in the Treasury' (P. 192-93). Later on, summing up the situation, he says: 'Since the Battle of *Karnal*, until *Nadir Shah's* Departure from *Shahjehanabad*, the Loss sustained by the Emperor and the People within and without the City, in Jewels, Treasure, Goods, Effects, and destroying of Fields, setting aside the Loss of the Buildings, amounted to very near one *Arrib*[1] of *Rupees*, out of which *Nadir Shah* carried away to the Value of 70 *crores*[2] in Jewels and other Effects; and his Officers and Soldiers 10 *Crores*.[3] The Charges of his Army, while he continued there, the Arrears, Pay and Gratuity advanced them, with what Goods were destroyed by Fire, and Fields laid waste, made near 20 *Crores* more.[4]

---

1 '125,000,000 *l*' (Footnote).

2 '87,500,000 *l*' (Footnote).

3 '12,500,000 *l*' (Footnote).

4 '25,000,000 *l*' (Footnote).

The Particulars of what *Nadir Shah* carried away with him:

	Crore
Jewels from the Emperor and *Omras*, valued at ...	25
Untensils and Handles of Weapons set with Jewels, with the *Peacock* Throne, and nine others set with precious Stones	9
Money Coined in Gold and Silver *Rupees*	25
Gold and Silver Plate which he melted down and coin'd ...	5
Fine Cloths and rich Stuffs of all Kinds ...	2
Household Furniture, and other valuable Commodities ...	3
Warlike Weapons, Cannon, etc. ...	1
	70[1]

(P. 219-21).

Hanway (*Travels*, II, 383) only copies, and slightly condenses, these details, and is therefore no independent authority.

Granting this estimate of Nādir's booty to be substantially correct, while money and bullion (with gold and silver plate) amounted

[1] The quotation ends here.

to 30 crores, the jewel treasure was valued at 40 crores and comprised 25 crores' worth of jewels (including the blackmail from the nobles), the rest being jewelled arms, articles, furniture and stuffs. Out of this 70 crores the value of some 5 to 10 crores may be the levy on the nobility, while the balance came from the *khiṣṣa* and the state treasuries.

These details of the treasure and their relative proportions are credible. There is just the advance on S̲h̲āh Jahān's treasure under all heads that one would expect after Aurangzeb's 50 years of careful management and simple habits.

In Mīrzā Mahdī Khān's *Tārīk̲h̲-i-jahān-kus̲h̲ā-i-Nādirī*, however, we read that Nādir S̲h̲āh obtained the equivalent of 15 crores from the state treasuries and through presents from nobles and governors from far and near (Edn. of 1265 *A.H.*, p. 207). This brief statement claims to give the total value of Nādir's booty, including the contributions from the aristocracy. In view of the low total figure and of the fact that no details are attempted we are disposed to attach more credit to Fraser's report, which has the air of an original and authoritative record.

While on the subject of Nādir S͟hāh's spoils we may remark that although a historian has no business to deplore transfer of wealth from one country or nation to another, and in fact may cheerfully grant that 'none but the brave deserve the fair' as well as the spoils of war, yet when a great country's entire artistic output extending over some two centuries of its best period is taken away at one blow, not to find a place in the secure vaults or show-cases of a palace or a museum, but the gold and silver articles of vertu to be melted into ingots, and the thrones, crowns, and jewelled furniture to be broken to pieces and distributed among the wild and hungry hordes of wandering shepherds and their descendants, not to speak of books, pictures, etc., which were probably used to feed the melting furnace or else thrown out on the streets as unworthy of the space they occupied—then the scandalized annalist may perhaps be forgiven if the limit of his patience is reached. Political vicissitudes have their horrors even for the denizens of the sequestered vale of art and letters.

INDEX

A

C.

D

G.

H.

I

K

L

M

S

T

U

V

W

Y

Z

THE MUGHUL INDIAN COURT AND ITS INSTITUTIONS.

A close-range survey of facts and details drawn from original Persian and contemporary European sources.

BY

ABDUL AZIZ, *Barrister-at-Law.*

In this Series the author has attempted a study of the Mughul court and the institutions connected with it, so as to obtain a tolerably clear picture of Mughul court life, and of the actual working in practice of the administrative system. In the opinion of the writer the spirit of this civilization can be better studied in the customs and manners of the people and in the systems and institutions in which they crystallized, than in the vicissitudes of kings and peoples which too often pass for " history ". The real life of a people is their social, intellectual and economic life, and this can be better studied in their manners and morals, their etiquette and procedure, their art and letters, than in the sequence of political events.

An attempt has been made to visualize the *milieu* which served as the cradle of Mughul thought and culture.

Books and pictures, buildings and furniture, arms, jewels and dresses, thrones and carriages, vessels and utensils—all articles of daily and occasional use in fact are passed in review, so as to give us an idea of the people's thought and life, taste and judgment, ambitions and achievements, and of public industry and royal patronage. Stirring scenes of Mughul court life—durbars and celebrations, receptions and progresses—are reproduced before the reader, and the glory of the Mughul past lives again.

Such a study of concrete facts will help us better to test the foundations of the social and administrative system of the Mughuls than theorizings and learned discussions based on conjectures and unverifiable hypotheses. We can see here how intimately pursuit of beauty and daily life were woven together in the better Mughul days, and how apparently unconnected currents of historical knowledge underlie, explain, and lead up to, the art and life of this great people.

It is expected that this series of monographs, when completed, will furnish material for a true social and economic history of Mughul India—indeed for a somewhat comprehensive history of Mughul Indian civilization.

The work is meant both for the scholar and the general reader; and an effort has been made to keep the style simple, clear and non-technical throughout; although here and there the specialized character of the subject made it a difficult task.

The Series comprises the following volumes, which are independent of one another:

(1) THE MANṢABDĀRĪ SYSTEM AND THE MUGHUL ARMY

The Mughul Court.

CHAPTER I.—The *Manṣabdārī* System or the "Military Aristocracy."—The Mughul Aristocracy as a social phenomenon.

CHAPTER II.—The Mughul Army: *Manṣabdārs* and their followers.—*Aḥadīs*.—The *Piādagān* or Infantry.—Artillery.—Estimate of the total strength of the army.

Ready in August, 1942.	Price	India	Rs. 2-8-0.
		Great Britain	4 sh.
		U. S. A.	1 $.

(2) THE IMPERIAL TREASURY OF THE INDIAN MUGHULS

Price	India	Rs. 8-0-0
	Great Britain	12 sh. 6d.
	U. S. A.	3 $

C

(3) ARMS AND JEWELLERY

PART I :—Insignia and Arms.

CHAPTER I.—Ensigns : *Chatr* (umbrella).—*Āftābgīr.—Kaukaba.* —*'Alam.—Chatrtoq, Tuman-toq* and *Qutās-toq* (yak-tail standards).—*Jandā.—Māhī-marātib* (fish ensign) and *Sher-marātib* (lion ensign).—Drum.—*'Aṣā* or stick (as sign of office).—Pen, Ink-stand and Pen-case (as sign of office).

CHAPTER II.—[illegible]: S[illegible] and [illegible]abres.—*Khānda* (straight sword).—*Dhūb* (anc[illegible] straight swor[illegible] Shield.—*Jamdhar* (broad dagger).—*Khanjar* ([illegible] da[illegible]ger).—[illegible]*k* (bent knife).—*Jambwa.—Katār* [illegible]ng and [illegible]ar[illegible] [illegible]-Knife.—Spear.—Bows and arrows.—Mace,—*Gupti* (sword-stick).—Walking-stick.

PART II :—Jewellery.

CHAPTER I.—Ornaments worn on the Emperor's person.

CHAPTER II.—Head-dress: Caps and crowns.—*Sar-pech, sar-band,* and *dastār-pech.*—Aigrettes and plumes (*jīgha, kalgī, turra*).—*Sihra* (bridegroom's chaplet or diadem).

CHAPTER III.—Necklaces and collars (*tasbīḥ, mālā, hār, larī 'aqd, urbasī, baddhī, dhukdhuki, gulū-āwez*).

CHAPTER IV.—Ornaments for hands and arms : Bangles and bracelets (*pahunchī, smaran, kara, dast-band*).—Rings.—*Bāzū-band* (armlet).

CHAPTER V.—Ear-drops and ear-rings (*latkan, jhumka, goshwāra, āweza,* etc.).

CHAPTER VI.—Miscellaneous : Gold tablets.—Watches.

Ready in September, 1942. Price

India	Rs. 3-8-0
Great Britain	5s.6d.
U. S. A.	1.50$.

(4) HORSE AND ELEPHANT TRAPPINGS AND OTHER CONVEYANCES USED BY THE INDIAN MUGHULS

CHAPTER I.—Horse Furniture: Silver, gilded, golden, plain gold, enamelled, and jewelled.—Furnished horses offered to emperors. Furnished horses bestowed by emperors (from Tīmūr to Aurangzeb). —Pictures.

CHAPTER II.—Elephant Furniture :—

Section I : Descriptive and illustrative :—Howdah.—'*Amārī*. —*Megh-dambār*.—Throne on an elephant.—Saddle.—*Jhūl*.—*Ankus*. —Miscellaneous.

Section II : Presentations :—Elephant furniture (*talā'ir*, *yarāq*, *sāz*) explained. Elephants with brass, silver, and gold trappings bestowed by emperors. Furnished elephants presented to emperors (from Akbar to Aurangzeb).—Pictures.

CHAPTER III.—Camel Furniture : *Kajāwa*.—*Muḥāfa*.—Saddle.

CHAPTER IV.—Conveyances :—

Section I : Wheeled carriages :—Bullock-driven vehicles.—Horse-driven vehicles.—*Bahal* or *Bahlī*.—*Rath*.—The English coach, etc.—Pictures.

Section II : Litters and sedans :—*Dolī*.—*Nālkī*.—*Pālkī* (palanquin).—*Takht-i-rawān*.—*Sukh-pāl*.—*Sukh-āsan*.—*Chauḍol*.—Pictures.

Section III: Boats :—The *Bajra* (budgerow).—War boats, etc.—Pictures.

Ready in November, 1942.	Price	India	Rs. 3-8-0
		Great Britain	5s. 6d.
		U. S. A.	1.50$

(5) THRONES AND FURNITURE, VESSELS AND UTENSILS

CHAPTER I.—Thrones and seats.

CHAPTER II.—Furniture: Tables.—Chairs and stools.—Cabinets.—Bed-steads.—Looking-glasses.—Braziers.—Statuary.

CHAPTER III.—Vessels and Utensils: Plates and dishes.—Cups and goblets.—Flasks, jars and jugs.—Trays and trenchers.—Rose-water bottle or fountain.—Scent-box (*'itr-dān*).—*Kāfūr-dān*.—Opium-box.—Betel-box.—*Chau-ghara* and *do-ghara*.—Spittoon.—Ewer and basin.—*Sifla-dān*.

Ready in December, 1942. Price

India	Rs.	3-8-0
Great Britain		5s. 6d.
U. S. A.		1.50$.

Orders and inquiries to be addressed to the Author:

ABDUL AZIZ, Bar-at-Law,
Qutab Road, Lahore (Punjab, India).

The following volumes are to follow at short intervals :—

(6) **THE IMPERIAL LIBRARY OF AGRA AND DELHI**

(7) **COURT AND CAMP (including the HARAM)**

(8) **ROYAL STABLES AND MENAGERIE**

For Selected Opinions see end of book.

SOME SELECTED OPINIONS

Dr. Sir Shafaat Ahmad Khan, Allahabad University, Allahabad. Now High Commissioner for India in South Africa.

My attention to Mr. Abdul Aziz's work was drawn by his excellent articles in the Journal of Indian History, Madras, in, I think, 1932 or 1933. I followed these articles with the greatest interest, as they dealt with an exceedingly difficult period in a style of striking lucidity and scientific precision. They contained none of the vague, obscure and inaccurate theories and facts which has sometimes impelled me to ask the author, why do you mumble ? I am glad to find that Mr. Abdul Aziz has collected together these articles and intends to publish them in a book form. I think it is a wise decision, and will be welcomed by all students of Mughul India.

Mr. Abdul Aziz's monograph on " The Imperial Treasury of the Greater Mughuls " is a work of solid research, sound judgment and great industry, and he has laid all students of the period under a deep debt of gratitude by his researches. Only those who have been through the novitiate of a trained historical scholar can appreciate the wealth and variety of the material he has collected together. His introductory chapter on the Imperial Household is excellent, and he has discussed the material with discrimination and tact. It does not pretend to be an exhaustive account, and he had perforce to content himself with the chief offices and departments....

Mr. Aziz then discusses the sources of revenue in the time of greater Mughuls and calculates their value, with his customary caution, detachment and precision.

The other articles deal with precious stones, and discuss the nature and quality of various kinds of stones, and trace the history of the Koh-i-Nur diamond. .... The section on Rubies is excellent while other sections that will appeal to readers are those on Ivory and Ivory Work in India . . . The chapter headed Actual Contents of Jewel Treasury from the invasion of Bābur to that of Nādir Shāh is a work of rare power,and should be read by all . . .

This brief analysis of a brilliant work will show at a glance how solid is Mr. Abdul Aziz's contribution to the knowledge of the Mughul India. Mr. Abdul Aziz's account of the Thrones, Chairs and Seats of the Great Mughuls makes fascinating reading, and there is a very fine account of the Peacock Throne. . . .

Mr. Abdul Aziz has also published articles on the Mansabdārī System and the Mughul Army. In these articles Mr. Aziz deals with a subject which has been the focus of acute controversy, and discusses the theories of Dr. Paul Horn, Blochmann, and others on the nature and origin of Mansabdārī.

The subject bristles with difficulties, and no writer can claim infallibility. I am, however, inclined to agree with the author that Dr. Paul Horn's whole account of the Man-abdārī System suffers from a fundamental misunderstanding. The author's explanation of the significance of Zat and Sawar ranks is plausible, as it represents a very dispassionate and thorough analysis of the works of previous writers on the subject. The reader will find Mr. Abdul Aziz's account of Mughul aristocracy as a social phenomenon interesting. . . .

In conclusion, I may add that few works published during the last twenty years have dealt so thoroughly and ably with an extremely important aspect of Mughul administration. Mr. Abdul Aziz's work is a pioneer undertaking and he has brought to his task all the qualities which are indispensable in a historian—sound judgment, care and caution in the handling of material, thorough study of the data and a lucid style. I am sure that the work will be welcomed by all students of this period with enthusiasm.

J. F. Bruce, Esq., University Professor of History, Panjab University, Lahore.

I have been rather closely aware, during the past eight years, of the studies of Mr. Abdul Aziz in Mughul history: and have read the published results with much interest. He is well equipped for the enquiries to which he has devoted himself for a good many years past, as he possesses not only an exact knowledge of Persian, but also a very wide and critical knowledge of the original contemporary sources from which alone a genuine understanding of that period can be derived. He has also a command of the language of French and German scholars of the subject.

Mr. Abdul Aziz is a very meticulous student, who insists upon a precise examination of the *minutiæ* of his subject, which gives his reader confidence in the originality and authenticity of his work. If he can give us a reflective summary of the result of his years of patient scholarship, he will make a valuable contribution to Indian history. He has, too, a clear and pleasant English style.

K. B. M. Afzal Husain, Vice-Chancellor, Panjab University.

Mr. Abdul Aziz has sent me for opinion reprints of his articles on various subjects connected with the history of the Mughul period. I have read these entertaining articles with great interest. Scientific precision regarding the authenticity of facts is the characteristic of these valuable contributions. The style is lucid and elegant. I have been struck by the extensive amount of labour which this study must have entailed and the thorough mastery of the subject which the author possesses.

So far history has been dealt with as the story of kings. Mr. Abdul Aziz has rendered valuable service to our country in dealing with the history of the people of the Mughul period. A king may be good or he may be bad, and to base the entire conception of the evolution of society on the personality of the king cannot historically .yield important results. The common people are the real material of which history is built, and I congratulate Mr. Abdul Aziz that he has constructed his story from such material.

Dewan Bahadur Dr. S. Krishnaswami Aiyangar, Editor, "Journal of Indian History," Madras.

Mr. Abdul Aziz, Bar-at-Law, Batala, Punjab, began rather a large scale history of perhaps the most brilliantperiod of the Mughul Empire in India, the empire under Shah Jahan. He contributed a series of articles as a preliminary to his work on the Manṣabdārī System of the Mughuls, and the Treasury and the Jewels of the Mughuls. In both of these subjects, he made a most thorough-going study of the topics he chose for treatment. Had he had the chance of completing the work without interruption, he should have succeeded in publishing a magnificent work on the Mughul Empire . . . . I may say that Mr. Abdul Aziz's work as a student of history deserves all commendation. I only hope that he will have, for this part of the work, such an encouraging reception as would stimulate him to go forward and complete the work, notwithstanding all the inconveniences, which his professional work as well as the other calls upon his time might interpose. I wish him all success in his enterprise.

The Hon'ble Sir Azizul Huque, Vice-Chancellor, Calcutta University, and Speaker, Bengal Legislative Council. Now High Commissioner for India in London.

I have gone through the reprints of your articles on the "Imperial Treasury and the Mughul Army" and I congratulate you on your careful collection of materials available in scattered works. I wish there were similar studies on the Mughul administration in India by other research workers.

S. H. Hodivala, Esq., Principal and Professor of History (retired), Bahauddin College, Junagadh, author of Historical Studies in Mughal Numismatics, Studies in Indo-Muslim History.

I am very greatly obliged to you for letting me see an advance copy of the Table of Contents of the Series of Monographs which you have projected on the Court and Institutions of the Indian

Mughuls. Your plan is an ambitious one and may take some years to complete but it is a task well worth performing and I devoutly hope that you will be able to complete it and get the extra treatises published, as you hope to do, during the next three years. To judge from the two dissertations which have been already printed, it is sure to be of great value for the intensive study of the subject. No one who has read those Essays on the Mansabdari System and the Imperial Treasury can fail to be most favourably impressed by your patient industry, wide knowledge of the original authorities, meticulous zeal and avidity for facts and the judgment and good sense you have brought to bear on the interpretation of the crabbed and frequently cryptic phraseology of the contemporary chroniclers. This is specially true of the disquisition on the Mansabdārī System—a subject which has been greatly perplexed by the guesses and theories of previous writers. It is possible that we shall never be able to understand it completely, but your elucidations of some of the obscure and controversial points may be justly described as honest and intelligent attempts to arrive at the truth and they deserve to be carefully considered by all earnest students of the subject.

Muhammad Shafi, Esq., Principal, University Oriental College, Lahore.

For many years Professor Abdul Aziz has been devoting himself almost entirely to a critical study of the problems connected with the history of Mughul India. His extensive reading of the original authorities of the first rank, with a judicious use of contemporary paintings and other illustrative materials has enabled him to give us a vivid and life-like picture of the Mughul times. His abundant sympathy with his subject, controlled by his critical capacity, has given his narrative the rare quality which is found only in the very best histories of the period. Students of the period will thank him for his deep researches into the period.

The late Mr. W. H. Moreland of the I. C. S., author of Jahangir's India, Agrarian System of Moslem India, etc.

It gave me great satisfaction to see that you had changed from the conventional style, which merely produces more "chronicles", and were trying to make history out of the chronicles and the other material available. . . . With all good wishes for the success of your work (Letter dated 31st January, 1933).

It is always pleasant to hear from anyone who is trying to find facts in Indian history, where so many people are content to make guesses (Letter dated 4th April, 1933).